GREAT SECTS

BY

ADAM

HUME KELLY

Great Sects with Dumbed Down Dogma
1st Edition
September 2005

Published by Eye Books Ltd
Colemore Farm
Colemore Green
Bridgnorth
Shropshire
WV16 4ST
Tel/fax: +44 (0) 845 450 8870
website: www.eye-books.com

Set in Gill Sans and Granjon by Snowbooks

ISBN: 1903070473
British Library Cataloguing in Publication Data
A catalogue record for this book is available from the British Library

GREAT SECTS

WITH

DUMBED DOWN DOGMA

BY

Adam Hume Kelly

EDITOR

Chris Davison

To, with and by

Mel

BFR

CONTENTS

CONTENTS

DEFINITIONS

Sect, n. A party in a Church, a nonconformist Church, any religious denomination, the adherents of a principle or school of thought. [F or L]

Dog'ma, n. (pl. -s, -ta). An article of faith or tenet esp. one laid down by ecclesiastical authority, the authoritative defining of what is to be believed, the body of beliefs so defined. [L f. GK, = tenet]

The Pocket Oxford Dictionary of Current English

INTRODUCTION

Great Sects with dumbed down dogma is a non-scholarly book containing a haphazard collection of facts, figures, fiction and trivia on many of the world's largest, smallest, oldest and strangest beliefs, faiths and religions.

AIMS

Whether for answering 'who, what, where' questions, general amusement, broadening the mind, as an aid to more informed after dinner conversation or indeed to pass a few precious moments, *Great Sects* should help.

CAVEAT

Great Sects is not inclusive, exhaustive or definitive on any or all subjects; it does however hope to be entertaining, informative and representative of a number.

Neither is it original, as all information has been painstakingly collected from sources readily available to all.

APOLOGIES

No offence intended or otherwise is meant to any of our subjects or readers. If any offence is caused, for whatever reason, we are very sorry.

In particular, the use of the word sect or sects is not meant in any way to be demeaning or derogatory. It is used as the dictionary definition would have it and for its obvious phonetic qualities.

THANKS

We would like to thank all who have helped with creating this book.

In particular the Sects themselves who, although they have had no direct input into the book, by their very existence in the public domain contribute to making the world of today the very 'rich tapestry' that it is.

On a much lesser note (and as promised) thank you to my godson Tom's father. Also Lee, Loubie, Steph, Cab and G for being the little rays of sunshine that they are, together with all at Eye Books especially Chris and Vic.

EVERYTHING YOU NEED TO KNOW ON A PAGE

Each of the sects' pages is identical in format, as below:

NAME OF SECT
LINK TO SIMILAR SECTS

- Vague denomination
- Rough date of origin
- Geography
- Estimated population
- Useful web address

Logo or symbol

History

The shortest history of...

Beliefs

A flavour of the beliefs of...

Points of interest

Snippets of interest, trivia, notables and related information.

Please note that dates are often suffixed by 'C' meaning century in the Christian or common era or 'BCE' meaning century before the Christian or common era.

THE SECTS

AETHERIUS SOCIETY

SEE HEAVEN'S GATE

- New Age Theosophical UFO Society
- 1955 UK, USA & elsewhere
- Aetherius from the planet Venus
- Maybe 1,000
- www.aetherius.org

HISTORY

'Dr' or 'Sir' George King, a London taxi driver, Master of Yoga and psychic, was told in May 1954 by Cosmic Master Aetherius that he was to become 'the voice of interplanetary parliament'. In July 1958 in Holdstone, Devon he was visited by Cosmic Master Jesus who transmitted the Twelve Blessings. King emigrated to America in 1960 and opened a centre in Hollywood. The Society has adherents on every continent.

BELIEFS

The Society is a cosmic evolution and spiritual path to enlightenment, where all science and religion merge. Extra-terrestrial contact is friendly and aimed at stopping further damage to Mother Earth. The law of cause and effect (Karma), spiritual progress and energy through service, radionic healing and reincarnation are all central tenets.

POINTS OF INTEREST

Twelve Blessings Include blessed is/are the peace-makers, wise-ones, lovers, planetary ones, thanksgivers, healers, Earth, Sun, Lords of Karma, Galaxy, Lords of Creation and Absolute.

Cosmic Voice Quarterly journal of the Society. ASIN: 000085A26.

23 November 1958 Cosmic transmission from Lord Karma that the next Master, in 'soft-topped shoes', is coming. Date unspecified.

Satellite No 3 Spiritual energy and contact increases when this Martian satellite nears Earth.

Operation Starlight Metaphysical operation to 'charge' 19 mountains with beneficial spiritual and cosmic energy.

UK magnetised peaks Holdstone and Yes Tor (Devon), Brown Willy (Cornwall), Ben Hope and Creag-An-Leth-Chain (Scotland), Coniston Old Man (Cumbria), Pen-y-Fan and Cardnedd Llwelyn (Wales), Kinderscourt (Derbyshire).

8 July 1964 'Primary Initiation of Earth' with energy.

UFO's First modern-day sighting was of nine flying saucers in 1947, by K Arnold in Washington, USA.

ALPHA COURSE

- Christian Teachings Charismatic
- 1977 London SW7 & worldwide
- Christian God
- 6 million and rising
- www.alphacourse.org

History

'The worlds most popular course on Christianity' was started in 1977 by Charles Marnham, a clergyman at the Anglican church of Holy Trinity Brompton, London. In 1990 Nicky Gumbel adapted the course into a beginners' guide to Christianity for non-believers. Since then its popularity has grown to such an extent that the 10 week, 15 session course now operates in at least 150 countries and 45 languages.

Beliefs

A series of 'meaning of life' talks that address the key issues relating to the Christian faith. Talk titles include Who is Jesus? Why did he die? How can I be sure? Why read the bible? Why and how should we pray? What about the Holy Spirit?, and more. A packaged programme that culminates, for some, in a belief in and even a visit from the Holy Spirit.

Points of interest

Order of service Faith, friendship and food, suppers and talks, ending in a weekend away in the countryside.

Lovebombing Or friendraising, the preferred method of unpressured recruitment.

HTB Holy Trinity Brompton, the 1826 'uninspired' Gothic church of architect Thomas Donaldson.

Toronto Blessing Charismatic event that occurred at Toronto Airport in January 1994 where an outbreak of Holy laughter, speaking in tongues and general Holy Spirit induced roaring has had far reaching influences.

Texts Questions of life: A Practical Introduction to the Christian Faith. Answers by N Gumbel. 1994 Christian book of the year.

Alpha First letter of the Greek alphabet used to denote God's eternity.

SW7 London's Knightsbridge, South Kensington and Queensgate.

ALPHA A is for Anyone interested in Christianity, L is for Learning and Laughter, P is for Pasta and Pie, H is for Help and A is for Ask.

Notable Ex-cabinet minister Jonathan 'I am a man of unclean lips' Aitken.

AMISH

- Christian Anabaptist-Mennonite
- 1693 Now only USA
- Christian God
- 130,000
- www.amish.net

HISTORY

Jacob Ammann, a 16C Swiss Mennonite (who were Anabaptists) founded the Amish to maintain those conservative Christian ideals that, he felt, were being lost to a corrupting world. They suffered persecution and, in the 1720's, many migrated to North America establishing agricultural communities in Pennsylvania, Indiana and Ohio. They continue to live an isolated anti-worldly communal lifestyle.

BELIEFS

The Old Order of 'The Plain People' does not accept the modern world. Inter-communal marriage only, no divorces, telephones, cars or electricity are accepted. All rules (Ordnung) are strictly adhered to, especially humility and holiness, and any miscreants are Shunned (Meidung). A New Order is more liberal, but remains non-resistant and pacifist.

POINTS OF INTEREST

Martyrs Mirror 16C book by TJ van Braght that outlines the suffering of early Christians, Anabaptists and Mennonites. Sometimes given as a wedding present.

'Went English' To abandon the faith.

Pennsylvania Dutch The language of the Amish. A mixture of High and dialect German.

Faceless dolls So as to avoid 'graven images' or idols as directed by Exodus 20.4. Also, no photographs.

Beards Left uncut after marriage. Moustaches are forbidden for being too military.

Baptism Informed adult baptism, upon formal enrolment to the Church at age 17-20. From the practice of the Anabaptists or 'rebaptizers'.

Feet washing A sign of humility and after Jesus Christ's washing of the Disciples' feet at the Last Supper.

Hats Black felt hats. Seniority indicated by size of brim.

Quilting Bees Gatherings where the Amish women make beautiful hand stitched quilts. An original C Jean Horst is art and investment.

Notables Oscar nominated film *Witness* starring Harrison Ford and Kelly McGillis.

ASATRU

- Norse Heathen Mythology
- 1970's N Europe, USA & Canada
- Odin, Thor & others
- Unknown
- www.thetroth.org

History

A modern reconstruction of the pre-Christian traditions of the warring Norse (aka Vikings) and Germanic peoples of Northern Europe. From Viking and Roman literature (Tacitus), folklore and local practice, interest in the Ancient Way awakened in 19C Europe. In 1972, Icelandic farmer and poet Sveinbjorn Beinteinsson founded Asatru, which is now an officially recognised religion in Iceland and growing.

Beliefs

Asatru, or Odinism to some, believes that the world exists as part of a cosmic ash tree of life (Yggdrasill). Humans reside in one of its roots (a middle earth) presided over by many gods and land/nature spirits (e.g. elves). A modern day virtue system includes: courage, truth, honour, fidelity, discipline, hospitality, self-reliance, perseverance and industry.

Points of interest

Odin Or Wodan or Wotan is the foremost of the Aesir (Sky Gods). The 'All Father', the 'Terrible Sovereign' and both the God of victory in battle and the dead of Asgard.

Mjolinir Thor's (God of Thunder) hammer and cricket bat by Newberry.

Valhalla Dead of battle escorted to the heavenly palace Valhalla, by the Valkyries.

Operatic anagram 'Ride of the Valkyries by Richard Wagner' rearranged to be 'a brave decent warrior, fly high, ride the sky'.

Berserkr State of berserk or a bear-skinned warrior.

Blot A ritual or ceremony, once a blood (blot) sacrifice, now more commonly the hallowing, sharing and offering of mead or similar drink.

Symbel A ritual toasting and drinking to the gods.

Runes North European alphabet, or Futhark, attributed to Odin and used for divination and fortune telling. Twenty-four 'letters' each with a name and meaning, in three rows of eight.

2005 Runic year 2255.

Notables Tuesday, Wednesday, Thursday, Friday after Norse Gods Tyr, Wodan, Thor and Freya/Frigg.

ASSEMBLIES OF GOD

- Pentecostal Evangelical Movement
- 1914 USA & now worldwide
- Christian God
- 51 million
- www.ag.org

History

Influenced by the 19C Holiness Movement and, in particular, Charles Fox Parham and William Seymour's Azusa Street Revival, the General Council of Assemblies of God was created in Hot Springs, Arkansas in 1914, under Eudorus Bell. From Springfield, Missouri it now encompasses over 200,000 churches in 191 countries and is the world's largest Pentecostal group.

Beliefs

A 1916 statement of 16 Fundamental Truths include faith healing and Baptism together with more traditional Protestant beliefs. This is now augmented by guidance on contemporary lifestyle issues and today's members can experience, as Jesus Christ's Apostles did, the Baptism of the Holy Spirit evidenced by the speaking in other tongues.

Points of interest

Acts 2 New Testament passage on 'the day of Pentecost' 'they were all filled with the Holy Ghost, and begun to speak with other tongues'.

1.1.1 1 January 1901, in Parham's Bethal Bible School, Agnes Ozman spoke in tongues signalling the dawn of Pentecostalism.

Lifestyle guidance No abortion, racism, homosexuality, pornography, suicide or gambling.

Mattersey Hall UK official bible college in Doncaster.

Disgraced Assemblies of God TV evangelists Jim Bakker and Jimmy Swaggart.

Pentecost Or Jewish Shabuoth is the 50th day or seventh Sunday after Easter.

312 Azusa Street Address in Los Angeles where in 1906 Seymour, the son of freed slaves, presided over 'Holy Ghost Bedlam'. Building demolished in 1931.

Pentecostal Evangel Official magazine with a weekly circulation of 215,000.

Missions 2,000 overseas missionaries from 27 in 1914.

Notables Elvis Presley sung in a Mississippi Assemblies of God choir, before publishing in 1954 his first single 'That's All Right, Mama'.

ATHEISM & AGNOSTICISM

SEE HUMANIST

- Non-Theistic Philosophy
- 1C BCE worldwide
- No god?
- Countless
- www.infidels.org/news/atheism

HISTORY

Since Epicurus of Ancient Greece (first Atheist), philosophers through the Ages have debated the existence and meaning of god. From the 18/19C writings of David Hume and Thomas Payne, to Ludwig Feuerbach (god is a human invention), Charles Darwin (evolution not creation), Friedrich Nietzsche (god is dead) and Charles Bradlaugh (militant Atheist MP), via Kant, Marx and Freud, arguments have continued.

BELIEFS

Broadly, there are two main Atheist schools of thought: Weak or Negative and Strong or Positive. The Weak has no belief that any god exists, i.e. negative belief. The Strong go further in believing that there are no gods, i.e. positive belief. Agnosticism, on the other hand, maintains there is not enough evidence to support the existence of gods.

POINTS OF INTEREST

Atheism Greek 'a' meaning without and theism, from theismos, for belief in god.

Psalms 14 'The fool has said in his heart, there is no God'.

Ernest Hemmingway 'All thinking men are atheists'.

Countries With largest Atheist populations, by percent, are: Germany, Slovenia, Russia, Israel, Netherlands, Hungary, Norway, Britain and New Zealand.

Anagram Crudely, Eat shit, he's a tit or 'hateist'.

Godparents Known as Mentors, Supporting Adults or Special Friends.

Charles Darwin 19C British naturalist (not naturist) who in his On the Origin of Species and The Descent of Man showed that through the survival of the fittest, species adapted from one generation to another and that man was a descendant of the apes.

Religion 'Is the opiate of the masses' (Karl Marx).

Agnostic Term coined by 'doubting' Thomas Huxley, the 19C British biologist, known as 'Darwin's bulldog'.

Notables The Invisible Pink Unicorn. A satirical goddess who, to Atheists, is as credible and provable as any deity.

BAHA'I FAITH

- Monotheistic Religion
- 1863 Iran, Israel & worldwide
- A God unknowable & indescribable
- 5 million
- www.bahai.org

History

In 1844 Siyyid Ali Mohammed (The 'Bab' or 'Gate' to Islam's Hidden Imam) foretold of the imminent appearance of God. In the 1860's Baha'u'llah (Glory of God) claimed he was the promised one and wrote the religion's Most Holy Book (Kitab-I-Aqdas). Succeeded by his eldest son (Abdu'l-Baha - Servant of God) then great-grandson (Shogi Effendi - Guardian of the Cause) and since 1963 the Universal House of Justice.

Beliefs

Baha'i will be the dominant faith uniting all others via the divine messages (manifestations) that mankind is yet to attain spiritual maturity. This requires an independent search for truth, oneness of human race with common language (English) and religion, equality of sexes, elimination of prejudice and no extremes of wealth/poverty.

Points of interest

Manifestations 'Prophetic cycle' has seen Adam, Noah, Abraham, Moses, Zoroaster, Buddha, Jesus, Mohammed, and Bab all as the precursors to the Baha'i Faith.

Practice Daily home worship. Feast every 19 days with prayer readings, administration and consultation. Annual 19 day fast 2-20th March. Pilgrimages.

Global The geographically most widespread religion in the world, after Christianity.

Abstinence Gambling, begging, alcohol, narcotics, homosexuality and partisan politics.

No 9 Is the single highest digit and is the number of openings in the human body and therefore an organising principal of the universe.

Calendar Based on solar year: 7 day week, 19 day month, 19 month year.

Afterlife Heaven and Hell are a state of soul. No reincarnation. Burial within one hour of death, feet to Acre.

Baha'u'llah "Earth is but one country and mankind its citizens".

Notables Cathy Freeman (athlete), Dizzy Gillespie (musician), David Kelly (MOD weapons expert).

BAPTIST WORLD ALLIANCE

- Christian Protestant Evangelical
- 1609 England & worldwide
- Christian God
- 31 million
- www.bwanet.org

HISTORY

The 1905 Baptist World Alliance is the umbrella organisation for the majority of all independent Baptist Churches. The founding of the Baptist movement is credited to Englishmen John Smyth and Thomas Helwys, although influenced by European Anabaptists and Reformation Separatists. In 1792 William Carey and the English Baptist Missionaries started mission work which remains central today.

BELIEFS

A range of beliefs, broadly Protestant, populate individual Churches. The beliefs that only actual believers should 'have the rite of passage' (baptism) to the Church and that each Church be independent of others, and free from interference by the State, distinguish them. Within each church there should also be equality of/between believers and ministers.

POINTS OF INTEREST

Character of the Beast 1609 book by Smyth claimed there was no support for infant baptism in the Bible.

St John the Baptist Baptised Jesus in the River Jordan and recognised him as the Lamb of God and Messiah. Saint of motorways and, unsurprisingly, baptism.

Baptistery The pool used for total immersion adult baptism. Trunks optional.

Package holidays Baptist, cabinet maker and temperance supporter, Thomas Cook, founded the first travel agency in Leicester in 1841. This was state owned from 1942 to 1972.

1st Amendment Of the US Constitution:'No law respecting an establishment of religion, or prohibiting the free exercise thereof' was influenced by the teachings of Baptist Roger Williams.

US Presidents Sometime Baptists of sorts: Harding (29th), Truman (33rd), Carter (39th) and Clinton (42nd).

Roger Williams In 1639 founded the first Baptist church in America in Providence, Rhode Island.

Notably absent 16 million Southern Baptists who left the World Alliance in 2004, over 'anti-American' thinking.

BENEDICTINE ORDER

See Catholicism, Jesuits & Franciscan Friars

- Christian Monastic Confederation
- 6C Rome & worldwide
- Christian God
- 8,000 monks & 16,000 nuns
- www.osb.org

History

The Order of St Benedict is a collection of autonomous monasteries, abbeys and convents whose patriarch was St Benedict of Nursia. The now oldest Western Monastic order thrived in the Middle Ages until the 16C Protestant Reformation dissolved many of the monasteries. Revived in the 19C, and 'confederated' by Pope Leo XIII in 1893, the order today has some 400 abbeys and 1,200 congregations.

Beliefs

The uniting code of the order is St Benedict's Rule. Written in low Latin in the 6C, the seventy-three chapters cover all aspects of spiritual and organised monastic life. In particular they include fear of God, no self-will, obedience, confession, selflessness, silence, humility, good works, manual labour, contemplation, punishments and hospitality.

Points of interest

Westminster Abbey The 'royal peculiar', now under the sole jurisdiction of the Queen, was originally built for the Benedictines by King Edward the Confessor.

Offshoots Cistercian (white monks) and Trappist orders.

Motto Pax or Peace.

The working day St Benedict ruled 5 hours of liturgy/prayer, 5 hours of manual labour and 4 hours of reading scripture make up the coenobitic/monastic day.

Cucumber sandwiches A variant of the original is cucumber, cream cheese and Benedictine liqueur.

CSPB Crux Sancti Patris Benedicti or Cross-of our Holy Father Benedict.

Black Monks So named after the black habit that is traditionally worn.

Liqueur Benedictine DOM is a brandy based herbal and fruit peel liqueur or elixir. Invented by Monks of the 16C Fecamp Monastery. DOM stands for Deo Optima Maxima or God Most Good and Great.

St Benedict Saint of poisoners and Europe. Feast day 11th July.

Notables Worth, Ampleforth and Downside Schools.

BRANCH DAVIDIANS

See Seventh-Day Adventists

The logo was a circular field filled with a star of David and twelve perimeter stars. "Ensign" was written across the center and the reference "Isaiah 11:1" was placed underneath it. Superimposed upon the design was a plant with three designations: Jesse the Stem, David the Rod, and Christ the Branch

- Christian Communal Doomsday
- 1929 USA
- Christian God
- 50
- www.sevenseals.com

--------------------------------- History ---------------------------------

Bulgarian Victor Houteff, an expellee from the Seventh-Day Adventist Church, founded the Shepherd's Rod movement (later the Davidian Seventh-Day Adventists under Ben Roden) and settled in Mount Carmel near Waco, Texas. In 1993 the commune was raided by the Bureau of Alcohol, Tobacco and Firearms, resulting in the deaths of leader David Koresh and eighty others. The reduced movement continues.

--------------------------------- Beliefs ---------------------------------

Strongly Adventist, followers believe in the accuracy of the Bible's Old Testament, especially the Book of Revelations, and in particular the imminent return of Christ. David Koresh was a prophetic Messiah who predicted that the 'endtime' or Armageddon would start in the USA. Sabbath on Saturday, vegetarian, no television, alcohol, caffeine or tobacco.

--------------------------------- Points of interest ---------------------------------

David Koresh Born Vernon Howell, he took the name David, as of the Biblical King David. Koresh, which in Hebrew means Cyrus, the Persian King who overcame the Babylonians in 539 BCE.

Spiritual wives Koresh, the Lamb from the Book of Revelations, introduced the New Light doctrine which made him the perfect mate for any follower he chose, so as to father a new line of God's children.

Seven Seals A Revelations scroll which predicts the date of Christ's second coming and the end of the world, locked with seven seals.

The Massacre In 1993 the 51 day siege of Mount Carmel (or Ranch Apocalypse) started over alleged illegal arms dealing and ended in a controversial fire, which has been the subject of an independent enquiry by Senator Darnforth.

Chevrolet Camaro 500HP muscle car owned by Koresh with 'Davids 427 Go God' engraved on the engine.

March 2012 The date for the end of the world.

Oklahoma bombing On 19th April 1995. By McVeigh, it was alleged as retaliation for the Waco massacre.

CARGO CULT (JON FRUM)

- Cargo Cult
- 1930's Tanna Island, Vanuatu
- Jon Frum
- Unknown
- www.enzo.gen.nz/jonfrum

HISTORY

The Melanesian Islands of the South Pacific have, since the 19C arrival of Europeans, been the home of many cargo cults. One such, Jon Frum, started in the 1930's on the Vanuatu island of Tanna. Influenced by World War II American troops and their 'cargo', the movement was declared a religion on 15th February 1957. Subsequent disaster relief programmes have reinforced this 'manna from heaven' cult.

BELIEFS

Ancient island beliefs centred on animism, ancestor worship and the exchange of goods and objects. With the western missionary influence and the bounty from the war a new belief system evolved. A happy world of plenty is anticipated after the return of the mythical Jon Frum and the ancestors who will sweep away the whites and bring much 'cargo'.

POINTS OF INTEREST

Cargo Any 'manna' of manufactured good that arrives by sea or air.

A Logic Cargo in boats and aeroplanes arrives as a consequence of building docks and airfields; therefore wooden replicas of the American troops' infrastructure will bring the cargo back.

Notables German Wislin of the Torres Straits, Vailala Madness of Papua New Guinea, Naked Cult of Espirito Santo, Masinga Rule of the Solomons and others.

Prince Philip HRH The Duke of Edinburgh is to some the Head of Cargo Supplies.

Signs from above A Red Cross sign and 'A gift from the people of America'.

Tanna South Pacific Island. One of the New Hebridian (now Vanuatu, meaning Land Eternal) 83 islands. Capital Porta Vila.

Cargo Cult's Two albums Alchemy and Vibrant.

Kava Narcotic drink prepared from the root of the Kava plant contributes to make Churchill's 'happy pagans of the island world'.

Jon Frum Also called John Broom, Kerapenmun (god of 1,084m mountain Tukosmeru) and King of America.

CATHOLICISM (ROMAN)

See Jesuits, Benedictine Order & Opus Dei

- 'Universal' Christian Religion
- 1C Vatican & worldwide
- Christian God
- 1 billion
- www.vatican.va

--- History ---

Catholicism is descended from the teachings of Jesus Christ's Apostles, in particular St Peter. Adopted by the Romans in the 4C, suffered a 'Great Schism' with the Orthodox church over Papal authority in the 11C, endured the 17C Reformation (which created Protestant-ism), Council of Trent, two Vatican Councils and 265 Popes, to become one of the world's oldest living institutions.

--- Beliefs ---

The Pope is the Apostolic successor of St Peter and is thus infallible; he is the supreme authority on the Gospel of Jesus. An all-male celibate priesthood teaches the seven signs of God (Sacraments): Baptism, Confirmation, Marriage, Ordination, Eucharist/Mass, Penance or Confession and anointing the sick lead to salvation. Virgin Mary is without sin and blessed.

--- Points of interest ---

Confession The contrite penitent confesses any mortal or venial sins to a priest, who issues prayer (Hail Marys), fasting or almsgiving as penance for absolution.

Transubstantiation Communion's bread and wine are the body and blood of Christ.

Peter's pence Annual (29th June) voluntary donation of the faithful to fund the Vatican. Credit cards accepted.

Christ's conception Immaculate.

12th March 2000 Day of Pardon and request for forgiveness by the Church for past violence and attitudes.

Bishop of Rome Aka Ratz, or God's Rottweiler is the first German pope for 900 years. Piano playing Bavarian Joseph Ratzinger or Pope Benedict (the Blessed) XVI, was born on 16 April 1927 and succeeded the Pole Karol Wojtyla or Pope John Paul II on 19 April 2005.

Mass Service of Worship, a weighty affair.

Holy See The 3.2 mile walled Vatican City is the smallest (0.44 square miles) state in the world, with a population of c.900.

Sinful Contraception, Homosexuality and abortion.

CHRISTADELPHIAN

- Christian Bible Believing Fellowship
- 1848 UK, USA & worldwide
- Christian God of the Bible
- Maybe 50,000
- www.christadelphian.org.uk

HISTORY

John Thomas, a London Doctor, was so traumatised by a rough crossing of the Atlantic that he vowed to dedicate himself to the discovery of God. The result was the founding of the movement in 1848. A convert, Robert Roberts, in 1898 amended Thomas' Statement of Faith and introduced fraternal gatherings. There is no central organisation, yet the movement now operates over 840 Ecclesias worldwide.

BELIEFS

The Bible is inspired, infallible and true Christianity is that of Jesus Christ's disciples. Some central Christian doctrines are adapted, including: God is a single entity not a Trinity; Jesus Christ was a human; the Holy Spirit as power of God only; Satan is a principle of evil rather than real and Man is mortal. Salvation through hope at a second coming.

POINTS OF INTEREST

Ecclesia   Or autonomous Church, where brothers and sisters meet in fraternal sober gatherings for the Breaking of Bread Service, with equal responsibility and no clergy.

Marquis Wellesley A 'fine fast sailing ship' which left St Katherine's Dock, London for New York on 15th May 1832 with Thomas as surgeon.

No Participation   in politics, voting, jury service, military or police service.

Hats and hair 'Let her be covered' and 'long hair, it is a glory to her'. St Paul's view to the Corinthians and still upheld by the sisters.

Delphians Advanced civilisation from Planet Gomoray in TV's Battlestar Galactica

Elpis Israel   Or Hope of Israel was Thomas' 1848 exposition on the Kingdom of God, with reference to the time of the end and the age to come. A central work.

Unrelated The John Thomas of DH Lawrence's Lady Chatterley's Lovers fame.

Christadelphian Meaning brother or brethren of/in Christ. The name was first registered to ensure conscientious objection and thus avoidance of the American Civil War of 1861-1865.

CHRISTIAN SCIENCE

- Christian Metaphysical Movement
- 1870's USA & now worldwide
- Christian God as principle
- Maybe 400,000
- www.christianscience.com

History

A new religious movement influenced by Phineas Quimby was 'discovered' by Mary 'Mother' Baker Eddy. Eddy cured herself of a serious back injury after reading Mathew 9.2 in the Bible. The Church of Christ, Scientist in Boston was founded in 1879. The Church, whose texts include the Bible, Eddy's Science and Health and the Manual of the Mother Church, now operates 2,000 branches in 80 countries.

Beliefs

Only the infinitely good God and the mind have reality. Sin, death, evil and sickness do not exist, other than in the mind, as they are patently not good. A healthy, happy, holy life can be attained through prayer. Prayer is the cure to all ills, not medicine, as the mind can heal any affliction. Spirituality, wellness and identity are central tenets.

Points of interest

Matthew 9.2 'They brought to him a man sick of the palsy, lying on a bed: and Jesus seeing their faith said unto the sick of the palsy; Son, be of good cheer; thy sins be forgiven thee'.

Palsy Paralysis, especially with uncontrollable tremors.

Hypnotism Animal magnetism or mesmerism is malicious, deceptive and leads to 'moral and physical death'.

Manual of the Mother Church 138 page book containing the bye-laws governing the structure, discipline and practice of the Church.

Science and Health with Key to the Scriptures This and the Bible are the 'dual and impersonal pastor' of the Church. 10 million copies sold since 1895.

Christian Science Monitor Daily newspaper of the Church and winner of seven Pulitzer prizes since 1908.

Practitioners Or 'journal-listed' healers earn by charging their patients/adherents.

Boston London 3,280 miles.

Notables 'Dear Lord, please don't let me fuck up'. Pre-launch quote by Alan Shepard, first American in Space, who was raised a Christian Scientist

CHURCH OF ALL WORLDS

- Neo Pagan Earth Religion
- 1962 USA, Australia & Europe
- Gaia, Holy Mother Earth
- Maybe a few thousand
- www.caw.org

HISTORY

The Church of All Worlds is one of the oldest and most influential Neo Pagan organisations and the first to attain exemption from US federal tax (1971). Influenced by Robert Heinlein's novel *Stranger in a Strange Land*, in 1962 Missouri, Tim Zell and Lance Christy founded the water-brotherhood Atl, which in 1968 became the current Church. Publishers of *Green Egg* magazine, the movement and its Nests continue.

BELIEFS

A Nature based religion that is 'dedicated to the celebration of life, the maximal actualisation of Human potential, and the realisation of ultimate individual freedom and personal responsibility in harmonious eco-psychic relationship with the total Biosphere of Holy Mother Earth'. Gaia's children (mankind) are responsible for stewardship of the sacred Earth.

POINTS OF INTEREST

Stranger in a Strange Land Fictional earthling and psychic Michael Smith is raised on Mars by Martians. He returns to Earth and 'explores human morality and the meaning of love'. A 1960's cult classic. ISBN No: 0441790348.

Nests Congregations.

Never Thirst A ritual of water sharing between friends in order to form water brotherhoods or kins. A symbolic act to remind one that water is essential to all life.

Grok Martian word to drink and be one. To wholly understand or empathise with.

Gaia Thesis A theology of deep ecology, published in 1970 by Zell, in that the Planet Earth is a single living organism and everyone is therefore her offspring.

'Thou art God' Greeting used to indicate the immanent divinity of all, as children of the Mother Earth.

Sex Positive, sacred & free.

Forever Forests Subsidiary organisation founded in 1977 by Gwydion Pendderwen to promote afforestation.

Annwfn 55 acre land retreat and faerie sanctuary in the Misty Mountains of Mendocino, California.

CHURCH OF COUNTRY SPORTS

- Ecumenical Politico Religion
- 2004 England & Wales
- Saint Hubert
- 12,000
- www.saint-hubert.org

HISTORY

Founded by R Brammer, V Gardner and J Milne as a result of the Government's Hunting Bill which threatened to ban hunting with hounds for fox, mink, and stag, together with hare coursing, in England and Wales. The bill which was forced through the House of Lords using the Parliament Act would, if legal and enforceable, end a centuries old way of life or religion in the eyes of the founders.

BELIEFS

Just as Saint Hubert took inspiration from a stag with a crucifix between its antlers, so current participants do from their sport. The countryside and the bounty it provides is the work of God and their activities bring them closer to the Creator. A ban would be an infringement of historic and traditional rights and freedoms, as afforded to other religions.

POINTS OF INTEREST

Saint Hubert The Apostle of the Ardennes who is the patron Saint of hunters, noted for his miracles. Feast day is 3rd November.

Vulpes vulpes Common fox, also known as Reynard, Charlie, Tod and Llwynog.

Red stag antlers A 'Royal' has 12 points/tines, an 'Imperial' 14 and a 'Monarch' 16. A Hummel has none at all.

Hunts 318 registered hound packs, with some 19,000 hounds.

Waterloo Cup Since 1836, the most famous annual (February) hare-coursing event, at the Altcar Estate.

John Masefield English poet who said hunting 'is a sport loved and followed by both sexes, all ages and all classes'.

Macnab A wild salmon, a brace of grouse and a red stag taken in one day.

Fadge 6 mph hound jog. Halloa: A rousing cry when a fox is seen.

Country sports Include hunting, shooting, stalking, angling, coursing, falconry and ferreting.

Notables Belvoir (1750), Berkley (12C), Cattistock (1806), Duke of Beaufort (1640), Pytchley (17C), Quorn (1855), VWH (1831).

CHURCH OF ENGLAND

- Christian Episcopal Anglican
- 1534 England & worldwide
- Christian God
- 70 million
- www.cofe.anglican.org

History

The established state church of England and the 'mother church' of the Anglican communion is descended from the 6C English Church of St Augustine and others. It split from the Roman Church and was created in law in 1534 by King Henry VIII by his Act of Supremacy during the divorce of Catherine of Aragon. Queen Elizabeth I influenced its current form and King Charles II, after the Civil War, settled its future.

Beliefs

'The Church of England is a broad church representing a wide spectrum of thought and theological practice'. Practical spiritual Christianity includes a belief in one God who created all, a Trinity, Jesus Christ as son of God, one life, 'Bible contains all things necessary for salvation', judgement upon death, heaven, hell and diversity as a virtue.

Points of interest

Anglican Community Present on every continent, 38 self-governing churches.

C of E Two Provinces of Canterbury and York control 43 UK dioceses, each with a cathedral, bishop and a see of archdeaconries, deaconries and parishes.

Lords Spiritual 26 Bishops sit in the House of Lords. Canterbury, York, London, Durham, Winchester and others by rotation.

No I First Archbishop of Canterbury in c.597, was St Augustine Apostle to the Angles (English), not angels, whose feast day is 26 May.

Primate 104th by divine providence of All England, the first peer and sometime poet, His Grace Rowan Williams of Canterbury.

BCP Thomas Cranmer's 1549 Book of Common Prayer. The standard for the majority since 1662.

Dating Easter The festival to celebrate Christ's resurrection is the first Sunday after the full moon following the Spring equinox (roughly 21st March), unless that full moon fell on a Sunday, in which case it is the next Sunday!

Notables Woman priests and gay American bishops.

CHURCH OF SCIENTOLOGY

- New Age Psychological Movement
- 1954 USA & worldwide
- L Ron Hubbard
- 8 million claimed
- www.scientology.org

History

Nebraskan L (Lafayette) Ron Hubbard published Dianetics: The Modern Science of Mental Health in 1950. Prompted by public interest, Hubbard founded what became the Church of Scientology in Los Angeles. The often-controversial movement has grown to have groups in 154 countries. Hubbard died in 1996 and was succeeded by David Miscavige who now heads a movement aiming to be less confrontational.

Beliefs

The subconscious or reactive part of the mind records painful physical or mental events as 'engams'. These negative engams clutter the subconscious affecting the fulfilment of potential in all 'Pre-clear' people. Dianetics and the Dianetic auditing of such engams results in the state of 'Clear' allowing the soul (Thetan) to reach its full potential.

Points of interest

'Operating Thetan' A state of soul above 'Cleared' that allows control over matter, energy, space and time (MEST) and thus immortality.

Hubbard 'Ideas not battles mark the forward progress of mankind'.

Battlefield Earth Science fiction book by Hubbard and film by Warner Bros starring John Travolta as Terl.

E-Meter Or Electropsychometer used to locate and audit areas of spiritual unrest in the Pre-clear person.

Freedom Magazine 'Investigative reporting in the public interest'.

Kobrigram Internet jargon meaning an unwelcome and threatening email or letter, named after Scientology lawyer Helena Kobrin.

Dynamics The eight urges or impulses which control all life are: self, sex, herd instinct, mankind, environment, universe, spiritual and infinity.

Miscavige Five foot five inch tall man and 4,867[th] 'Cleared' soul, who runs the Religious Technology Centre, which controls the Church.

Alleged Notables Tom Cruise, John Travolta, Kirstie Allie and Lisa Presley.

CHURCH OF SCOTLAND

- Christian Reformed Presbyterian
- 16C Scotland
- Christian God
- 600,000
- www.churchofscotland.org.uk

History

The 16C Protestant Reformation and the teachings of John Calvin in Geneva influenced John Knox to reform Scotland from its Catholic 'idolatry'. The Revolution Settlement of 1690 finally secured the position of the Church that, despite occasional division and English interference, it maintains. 'Reformed and Presbyterian, national but free', The Kirk of Scotland is the world's only Presbyterian national state church.

Beliefs

Scottish Presbyterians are Protestant Christians so the authority of the Bible is paramount, together with the 17C creedal Westminster Confession of Faith. The Reformed tradition states that God predetermines salvation regardless of human effort. All encapsulated by 'What is the chief end of man?' 'Man's chief end is to glorify God and to enjoy Him forever'.

Points of interest

Presbyterian Greek elder.

Kirk Scottish church from Old Norse. Captain James Tiberius no relation.

Courting Local Kirk session courts, to district presbytery courts, to a national General Assembly; all noted in the Moderator's Blue Book.

Logo Cross of St Andrew behind a burning fire. St Andrew's decussate cross, cloud white on sky/azure, or Pantone 300 blue.

30th November 60 St Andrew's crucifixion is not a public holiday in Scotland.

Nickname Frozen Chosen.

Calvin John 1509-64. French theologian, reformer, sometime 'Dictator of Geneva' and author of the influential Institutes of the Christian Religion.

Knox John 1505-72. Scottish reformer responsible for the line 'One man with God is always in the majority'.

Influences Saints Ninian (1st UK Christian in 4C) and the Irish Columba of Iona (5C Christianity and the bringer of Uisge or whiskey).

Calvin Not the Kelvin's temperature scale, where absolute zero or 0K is 'so cool' that molecular energy slows.

CONFUCIANISM
SEE TAOISM & ZEN BUDDHISM

- Religion of social propriety
- c.500BCE China, Korea & Japan
- Maybe 155 million
- www.confucius.org

HISTORY

A Chinese 'scholarly tradition' of moral, social, political and religious ideology 'revived' by the 'lover of the ancients' Confucius in c.500BCE. The Han Dynasty (206BCE-220) adopted it as the official state philosophy; the Sung Dynasty (960-1279) gave us Chu Hsi, his Sze Shuh (four books) and Neo-Confucianism. Confucianism's influence continues despite the 1949 Peoples' Republic and the Cultural Revolution.

BELIEFS

A Confucian should be a saint, scholar and gentleman in a harmonious world of piety and respect, religious ritual and righteousness. The Golden Rule of 'do not do unto others what you would not want others to do unto you' underpins the Confucian way of life. Life passages, virtues and learning to be human are all part of the ultimate 'embodiment of good'.

POINTS OF INTEREST

Confucius Or more properly K'ung Fu-Tze (Kung the Master) was born in 551BCE 'a child as pure as crystal' 'to become a king without a kingdom'. Died 479BCE.

Final words 'The Sacred Mountain is falling, the beam is breaking. The wise man is withering away'.

Mandarin Orange bureaucrat ducked official language.

Virtues Benevolent Jen, manners of Li, righteous dutiful Yi, trustworthy Hsin and wise Chih.

Duty Summed up as 'The father must be a father and the son a son'.

Sze Shuh Four later books assembled by the Neo 'great ultimate' Chu Hsi which include the Analects.

Analects Or Lin Yu, the recorded sayings or conversations of Confucius.

'Confucius says' Man who walk through airport turnstile sideways going to Bangkok!

Last word and motto 'Requite injury with justice and kindness with kindness'.

6 Classics The Confucian canon of the Book of Changes, of Odes, of History, of Rites, of Music and the Spring and Autumn Annals.

DREAMING/DREAMTIME

- Aboriginal Mythology
- Australia & Torres Strait Islands
- 410,000
- www.dreamtime.net.au

History

Hunter-gatherer Aboriginals arrived in Australia from Asia some 40,000 years ago. Unaffected by any technological advance they had the longest cultural history of any people until 1788 and British colonisation. Under the British and then the 1901 Federal Government, the Aboriginals suffered very great discrimination. Recent changes to the law (voting, land and human rights) have started a process of reconciliation.

Beliefs

Dreaming or Dreamtime is a Western approximation for an evolved and complex unwritten set of faiths, practices, laws, events and knowledge. This collective memory and identity relates to the creation of the (their) natural and sacred world by ancestor beings and spirits. All natural things have a meaning, significance, life and connection with the past.

Points of interest

Totem Each person has an individual 'dreaming' and is born with a totemic identity. Normally an animal or plant, e.g. a 'cold and slow raven' person like a 'stupid bustard'.

Rainbow serpent Pythonesque creator of man and God of fertility.

The Song Lines Lines of communication and a book by Bruce Chatwin.

Captain Cook Claimed Australia for Britain in 1770 aboard the Endeavour, a Whitby coal ship.

Bloodletting Or blood sacrifice, including male and female circumcision.

Sacred site The colour changing 345m monolithic sandstone rock Uluru or Ayers Rock.

Altjira Sky God with emu's feet and three large toes.

Mekigar or Karadji A clever, psychic or medicine man. A shaman.

Infamous Past official policies: 'terra nullius' (land belonged to no one), 'pacification by force' and 'urban assimilation'.

Rock art Often in ochre, expressing myth and ritual. At 17,000+ years old the Bradshaw paintings of Kimberley are the world's oldest.

DRUIDRY

See Wicca

- Pagan Celtic Spirituality
- Maybe 3C BCE UK, Europe & USA
- Many Gods and Goddesses
- Unquantifiable
- www.druidnetwork.org

History

Druids, a privileged class of ancient Celt, were divided into three groups, Druids (philosophers), Bards (poets), and Ovates (prophets). Julius Caesar and the Romans largely destroyed the entire order. In the 18th and 19th centuries, revivalists John Aubrey, John Toland and William Stukeley (antiquarian authors), William Blake (poet) and Lola Morganwg created the basis for today's many and varied neo-Druid groups/groves.

Beliefs

Ancient Druidry was unwritten, with only Caesar's and Pliny's writings being of any record. The modern traditions therefore rely on myth, archaeology and the Irish sagas for custom and practice. Common themes are reverence of the earth and nature, belief in the Awen force, an immortal soul and serious ceremonial celebration of seasonal festivals.

Points of interest

Awen The inspiration or flowing spirit central to Druidry which is symbolised by three rays of sunlight and used as a mantra by many.

Druid human sacrifice According to the Romans yes. Less practised today!

Solstice Sun at highest or lowest points during the year. Summer solstice (Alban Hefin) 21st June and Winter solstice (Alban Arthan) 21st December.

Equinox Day and night of equal length. Vernal equinox (Alban Eilir) 21st March and Autumnal equinox (Alban Elfed) 21st September.

Druid From Gaelic word duir, or similar, meaning oak tree. The oak (quercus spp) was important not least because it joined the earthly kingdom to the sky kingdom

Fire festivals Imbolc (1st February), Bealtane (1st May, Mayday), Lughnasadh or Lammas (1st August, Harvest), and Samhuinn (1 November).

Mistletoe Or Holy Bough, the aerial parasite and modern alternative cancer cure. Golden sickle and fresh breath vital.

Venues Stonehenge (bluestone) and Avebury (sandstone) circles in England.

ECKANKAR

- Religion of Light & Sound
- 1965 USA & worldwide
- Sugmad
- 50,000
- www.eckankar.org

History

Paul Twitchell in 1965 claimed he was reviving an ancient faith of the Order of Vairaga Masters, which had been passed to him by the 500 year old Tibetan monk and ECK Master, Rebazar Tarzs. Twitchell declared himself the 971st ECK Master and founded the organisation in California. Succeeded in 1971 by Darwin Gross (972) and in 1981 by Sri Harold Klemp (973), the now Minnesota based movement prospers.

Beliefs

The cosmic current, or ECK, of Light and Sound is the holy spirit and voice of Sugmad, Hu, It or God that 'sustains all life'. Spiritual 'unfoldment' and growth, 'God-Realisation' and good Karma as a 'co-worker with God' are attained by experiencing the ECK through spiritual exercises, dream, the chanting of mantras and soul travel.

Points of interest

Mahanta Harold Kemp the living manifestation of God, a prophet and spiritual leader.

Soul travel 'To ride the waves of divine love'. A separation of body and spirit, or a shift in consciousness, allowing the exploration of God's 12 planes or worlds. Considered quite different to astral travel/projection.

Spiritual exercises 20 minutes a day to 'build spiritual stamina'. The simplest is to clear the mind and repeatedly sing the word Hu.

22nd October Spiritual new year and 1965 founding day.

Chela A spiritual student or pincer like organ or claw.

Hu An ancient name of God.

Shariyat-ki-Sugmad Or Way of the Eternal is Paul Twitchell's book and authoritative text for the religion. 'A unique perspective on the spiritual history of humanity and its relationship to God and Spirit'. Anon.

Unrelated ECKy thump! Northern slang loosely meaning Good God. Or a Lancastrian martial art, invented by the Goodies, of Goodie Goodie yum yum fame.

ECK The life stream of the holy spirit is seen as light or heard as sound.

ELVIS RELIGION

- Presleyanity or Elvisism
- 1935 USA & worldwide
- The King
- Unknown
- www.elvis.com

History

Elvis Aron or Aaron Presley, born 8th January 1935 in Tupelo Mississippi, was a rock idol and one of 'pop' music's greatest influences on world culture. He died at home (Graceland) on 16th August 1977, aged 42. His life, memory and alleged subsequent sightings have spawned the First Presleytarian Church of Elvis the Divine, First Church of Jesus Christ Elvis and the Church of Two Elvises amongst others.

Beliefs

'For unto you is born this day in the city of Memphis a Presley, which is Elvis the King'. A Messianic figure who inspired millions to abandon the austerity of the 1950's and embrace the 'Young and Beautiful' 1960's. Rockabilly religious parody includes 8th January as a holy day, prayer facing Las Vegas, Graceland pilgrimage, dietary rules and overindulgence.

Points of interest

AKA Hillbilly Cat, The King or Father of Rock 'n Roll, Elvis the Pelvis and The King.

Elvis lives Urban myth of chip shop, supermarket and the like sightings.

Texts One night in the Heartbreak Hotel, viva Las Vegas, wearing blue suede shoes with my poor boy fool hound dog, who is all shook up because the green green grass of home and his good luck charm are way down my way across the blue river in the moody blue promised land of jailhouse rock and a hard headed woman. 17 hits.

Last single Way Down, '77.

Quote 'Rhythm is something you either have or don't have, but when you have it, you have it all over'.

Graceland 14 acre mansion including Meditation Garden in Memphis Tennessee, off Elvis Presley Boulevard. Now open to the public attracting around a million visitors every year.

Stamps 46 countries have issued postage stamps of Elvis. Grenada first in 1978 and the USA in 1993 (above).

No 1 Nike and Dutch Junkie XL's (now JXL) remix of 'A Little Less Conversation' and a lot more football in 2002.

FALUN GONG

- Chinese Spiritual Discipline
- 1992 China & worldwide
- Li Hongzhi
- 100 million claimed
- www.minghui.org

History

In 1992 Li Hongzhi began publicly teaching a previously secret form of spiritual exercise in Northern China. The popularity of this discipline grew until, in April 1999, 10,000 practitioners staged a demonstration in Beijing against the Chinese Government's treatment of spiritual organisations. China banned Falun Gong in July 1999 although the movement continues to prosper and receive support worldwide.

Beliefs

An amalgam of certain Buddhist, Confucian and Taoist doctrine that focuses on self-cultivation of mind, body and spirit through the practice of Quigong. A belief that, through exercise and meditation, spiritual enlightenment and control over life, illness and death can be realised. Truth, compassion and forbearance are the virtues required for moral character.

Points of interest

Quigong The practice of refining mind, body and spirit through exercise. Especially cultivating the ability to centre one's energy in the lower abdomen.

Text The Zhuan Falun.

Five disciplines Buddha Showing a Thousand Hands, Falun Standing Stance, Penetrating the two Cosmic Extremes, Falun Heavenly Circulation and Strengthening the Divine Powers.

13th May The Buddha Siddharta Gautama's birthday as well as that of Li Hongzhi, although the Chinese authorities dispute the latter.

Symbol The 'design is the universe's miniature, and in all other dimensions it has its forms of being and its evolution processes, so I call it the world'. Hongzhi.

Spinning swastika Represents an energy vortex.

Xiejiao The teaching of falsehoods or superstitions by cults; the Atheist Communist Chinese Government's view of many.

Aliens Hongzhi has stated that aliens 'want the human body'. The James Randi Foundation is offering a million dollars for proof of any paranormal power.

FINDHORN COMMUNITY

- New Age Spiritual Holistic Community
- 1962 Nr Inverness, Scotland
- Thousands
- www.findhorn.org

History

New Age, a term first used by Theosophist Alice Bailey, defined a new spiritual age or Age of Aquarius. In 1962, Spiritualists Peter and Eileen Caddy, with Dorothy Maclean who was able to contact the nature spirits (Devas), planted a vegetable garden. So 'unnaturally' successful was the garden that it attracted great publicity. The Foundation today is a learning centre for personal and spiritual transformation.

Beliefs

The Foundation, Community and Ecovillage state that they 'believe that humanity is engaged in an evolutionary expansion of consciousness; they seek to develop new ways of living infused with spiritual values' and their 'work is based on the values of planetary service'. One people, one world, one destiny in an enlightened model democratic community.

Points of interest

Game of Transformation Commercial board game where a 'personality marker is moved along a life path' starting at the Physical level and moving through Emotional, Mental and Spiritual levels.

Residential courses From Spiritual Practice, Astroshamanic Healing and Soul Retrieval to Dance Rituals, Symbols and many more.

Angel cards Messages from the 'inner companions' (Angels) in a 52 card set.

Opening Doors Within Eileen Caddy's book with a meditation for every day.

David Spangler One time American Theosophist who, in the 1970's, helped define Findhorn's spiritual education programme, the University of Light.

Sacred dances Communal circle dances for celebration.

Ecovillage One of the Global Ecovillage Network of sustainable settlements.

Outstanding 40lb cabbages.

Theosophical Society New Age movement of East meets West secret wisdom, founded in 1875 by Helena Blavatsky and sometimes described as 'the Clapham Junction for the occult'.

FRANCISCAN FRIARS

See Benedictine Order

- Christian Ascetic Religious Order
- 1209 Rome and worldwide
- Christian God
- Unknown
- www.wtu.edu/franciscan

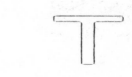

History

St Francis of Assisi founded three Franciscan orders, all of which exist today. The order of Lesser Brothers or Friars Minor, the first. The second, with St Clare in 1212, was the order of Poor Ladies or Poor St Clare's. The third or Tertiary order, in 1221, of Brothers and Sisters of Penance, for lay followers. Differences over the definitions of poverty and ownership led the first order to divide into another three orders.

Beliefs

Inspired by a biblical sermon, Francis set out to imitate certain aspects of Jesus Christ and his life, of which absolute poverty and non-ownership were key. Although viewed differently by each of the sub-divisions, the rule of poverty remains central. The itinerant Friar relies on alms to sustain the prayer, preaching and penance that are undertaken.

Points of interest

Mendicant Someone who lives by begging as do some Franciscan orders as well as the Carmelite, Augustinian and Dominican Friars.

Lesser Brothers Divided into the observant Friar Minors, the Conventuals and Capuchins orders.

Grey friars So named because of their ash grey habit. Today though mostly brown.

William 'Billy' Bunter 'The fat owl of the Remove' was a boy at Greyfriars School in Frank Richard's books.

Assisi Town of c.25,000 in Umbria, Italy. 'Giotto' see Giotto's frescoes/paintings.

Frank Meaning candid and open, from the Latin Francus.

St Clare Canonised in 1255 and now the patron saint of Television and Goldsmiths.

Roger Bacon Or Doctor Mirabilis was a 13C Franciscan from Ilchester, Somerset, who invented the magnifying glass and a process for making gunpowder.

Tau Or St Anthony's cross was adopted by St Francis. Representing the fifteenth and last letter of the Hebrew alphabet, which symbolises the Cross of Jesus. The Friars' habit is T shaped, making them 'walking crucifixes'.

FREEMASONRY

- Fraternal brotherhood
- 1717 UK, USA & everywhere
- Great Architect of the Universe
- Maybe 6 million
- www.grandlodge-england.org

History

Perhaps descended from the stonemasons of King Solomon's Temple or the Pyramids, modern organised freemasonry is credited to the formation in 1717 of the first Grand Lodge in London. It is a product of the 18C unions of 'free superior' skilled medieval masons allowing non-masons membership of the Craft. Accepted rather than operative Freemasonry has become the world's best known secret society.

Beliefs

'A society of men' whose 'members are taught its precepts by a series of (secret and elaborate) ritual dramas, which follow ancient forms and use stonemasons' customs and tools as allegorical guides'. A religious institution rather than a religion that believes in a 'Supreme Being', whose brothers are joined through mutual help, fellowship, love, relief and truth.

Points of interest

Ancient and Modern The two strains of masonry united as the United Grand Lodge in 1813.

HRH The Duke of Kent is the current Grand Master of the United Grand Lodge.

3 degrees Of spiritual wisdom and qualification are Entered Apprentice, Fellow Craft and Master Mason.

2 rites Having completed Craft lodge masonry a Master Mason may pursue by degree the York or Scottish rites.

3 Great Lights Or furniture of the lodge: the volume of sacred law (open Bible), a square and a compass.

Handshake Most commonly is thumb pressed into joint of forefinger where it joins the hand.

Magic Flute or Freemason opera of 1791 by Mozart with 3 cords, 3 ladies and 3 doors to the Sun Temple.

Boaz and Yachin The two pillars of King Solomon's Temple, named by Hiram Abif the Masons' mason.

No connection The famous Square and Compass pub in Worth Matravers, Dorset.

Square and Compass Representing fair and square behaviour within the bounds of the compass.

HEAVEN'S GATE

See Aetherius Society

- UFO Doomsday Cult
- 1973 USA
- Ti & Do or Bo & Peep or The Two
- Nil
- www.heavensgate.com

History

The Human Individual Metamorphosis, Total Overcomers Anonymous and latterly Heaven's Gate was founded in 1975 by Marshall Herff Applewhite (Do) and Bonnie Lou Nettles (Ti). Numbers fluctuated before, in March 1997, thirty-nine of the main 'groundcrew' committed suicide, in San Diego, California, in order to leave their 'physical containers' and join a space-ship hiding behind the comet Hale-Bopp.

Beliefs

2,000 years ago extra-terrestrials from a literal and physical Kingdom of Heaven visited earth, as told in certain Biblical passages, especially Revelations, and 'incarnated' the body of Jesus. Earth is ultimately evil, corrupt and doomed. Applewhite/Do was the leader of the evacuation party to a gender free sexless eternal life in 'The Level Above Human'.

Points of interest

Higher Source   The name of the web designer company run to help fund the group.

Hale-Bopp   Or Comet C/1995 01 (Hale-Bopp) was discovered in 1995 by Alan Hale and Thomas Bopp. A nucleus of ice, dust and rock, surrounded by a coma of steam, orbiting the Sun at 27 miles per second became visible to the human eye in the late 1990's. Now only visible from the Southern hemisphere with a large telescope.

Castration   Of the dead (21 women and 18 men) 8 of the men had undergone voluntary castration in readiness.

Earthstation   The mansion at Rancho Sante Fe, complete with swimming pool, tennis courts, putting green and sauna reportedly sold in 1999 for $668,000.

Exit press release   Released on 22nd March 1997 by the group on their website, stated that their 'earthly task' was done and that the 'away team' had taken the 'leap of faith' 'out of death' to the 'next level'.

Apple sauce   Mixed with the sedative Phenobarbital and washed down with Vodka, followed by suffocation with a plastic bag, was the method of 'closure'.

HINDUISM—SANATANA DHARMA
See Vaishnavism, Shaivism & ISKCON

- The Indian religion
- 3,000BCE Indian subcontinent
- Brahman World Spirit
- 900 million
- www.hindunet.org

History

Hinduism, or the Eternal Law of many paths to one truth, is an evolving religious tradition, a philosophy and way of life of varied beliefs, practices and scriptures. Hinduism has developed from and via the original Indus Valley civilisation, the Aryan invasion, the Vedic traditions and scriptures, to the breakaway of Buddhism and Jainism. Vaishnavism, Shaivism and Saktism are the major groupings of a myriad of others.

Beliefs

To be born a human is a rare opportunity to advance towards liberation (Moksha). The moral, traditional and scriptural law of Dharma underpins a Karmic cycle of suffering and reincarnation, with a quest for liberation through works, knowledge, meditation and devotion. Four stages (Asramas) of life with goals of pleasure, wealth, duty and release.

Points of interest

Hindu Name derived from the Sanskrit for river, Sindhu and referring to the river Indus (now in Pakistan). Not to be confused with the holiest of all rivers, the Ganges.

Vedas The Rg, Sama, Yajur and Atharva Veda are the heard scriptures of the Indo-European Aryans, which together with other remembered epics, make up the wealth of Hindu scripture.

Diwali Festival of lights, the triumph of light over dark.

Caste Priestly Brahmins, ruling Kshatriyas, trading Vaishyas, servant Shudras and untouchable Harijans.

A prayer 'Lead me from the unreal to the real; lead me from darkness to light; lead me from death to immortality'.

Nepal Only Hindu state.

Aum Or Om. The symbol or sound of the infinite. The essence or seed of all mantras.

Big 3 of very many Brahma, red God of Creation, Vishnu, the Preserver and Shiva, the auspicious Destroyer.

Asrama Vedic way of student, house builder, forest dweller and renouncer.

Moksha Liberation from the cycle of death and re-birth.

Notable The sacred cow.

HUMANISM

SEE ATHEISM & AGNOSTICISM

- Philosophical Secular 'Naturalistic'
- 20C worldwide
- Maybe 15% of world's pop
- www.iheu.org

HISTORY

Modern secular Humanism is a 20C movement that encompasses most atheists and agnostics, 'rejects all supernaturalism and relies primarily upon reason and science, democracy and human compassion'. It evolved from the writings of ancient philosophers, via the Middle Age Renaissance, the 17C Enlightenment and 19C Freethinkers to the 1933 publication of a Humanist Manifesto by 34 leading humanists.

BELIEFS

In the words of Kurt Vonnegut 'being a Humanist means trying to behave decently without expectation of rewards or punishment after you die'. Humanism is a positive informed 'lifestance' aimed at achieving personal fulfilment through an active ethical attitude and philosophy. The welfare of humankind and the physical world is all that matters.

POINTS OF INTEREST

Holy Trinity   Of science is reason, observance and experience.

Celebrant & Officiant   'Celebrant' weddings and 'officiant' funerals.

Darwin Day   Movement to establish 12th February 2009 as a day of 'global celebration' marking the 150th anniversary of the publication of his book On the Origin of Species.

Catch 22 'How much reverence can you have for a supreme being who finds it necessary to include such phenomena as phlegm and tooth decay in his divine system of creation'. J Heller.

Socrates Greek philosopher, wisest man of the ancients and father of humanism, who drank hemlock.

Humanist of the Year Awarded since 1953. Margaret 'Handmaid's Tale' Atwood the 1987 winner.

Pink Triangle 1992 UK charitable trust for the arrangement of gay and lesbian affirmation ceremonies.

Humanism Forms of: Christian, Cultural, Literary, Modern, Philosophical, Renaissance, Religious and Secular.

Notably absent A humanist contribution to BBC Radio 4's Thought for the Day.

ISKCON HARE KRISHNA

SEE HINDUISM, SHAIVISM & VAISHNAVISM

- Hindu Devotional Denomination
- 1965 The West & now India
- Krishna
- Not available
- www.iskcon.org

HISTORY

AC Bjaktivedanta Swami Prabhupada founded the International Society for Krishna Consciousness in America in 1965/6. The movement's philosophy originates from the 16C Gaudiya Vaishnavism of Sri Caitanya. Prabhupada was solely responsible for the now worldwide confederation of over a hundred temples, farm communities and institutes. Initially in America and the West, the organisation is flourishing in India.

BELIEFS

An ascetic simple living and 'high thinking' communal organisation that believes in the ecstatic devotion of Bhakti-yoga, or discipline of devotion, to Krishna, an emanation of the God Vishnu. The aim is to attain permanent 'consciousness' for the soul, together with salvation from the wheel of Hindu death and rebirth, with a return to the Godhead.

POINTS OF INTEREST

Mahamantra Hare Krishna Hare Krishna Krishna Krishna Hare Hare Hare Rama Hare Rama Rama Rama Hare Hare. The great mantra.

Hare Meaning devotional pleasure or energy.

Krishna Name of God, the all attractive.

Rama Name of God, the supreme pleasure.

No Violence, illicit sex, gambling or intoxicants.

Internet radio At www.chantandbehappy.com the Radio Krishna Network.

Back to Godhead Magazine printed six times per annum.

Conscious practice Reading, chanting, friendship and remembering.

Favourite colour Orange!

Notables Reportedly George 'all you need is love' Harrison, The Grateful Dead and poet Allen Ginsberg.

Country seat Bhaktivedanta Manor in Hertfordshire, donated by Harrison in 1973. A school and Krishna Temple. Formerly Piggots Manor.

Bhagavadgita Or song of the Master. 200BCE 700-verse poem in which Krishna councils warrior Arjuna over bhakti (devotion). Prabhupada 'as it is' translation key.

ISMAILI AGA KHANIS

See Sunni, Shia, Sufi, Wahhabi, Nation of Islam

- Islamic Shia Minority
- 765 Asia, Africa, Europe & America
- Allah & The Aga Khan
- 20 million
- www.iis.ac.uk

History

In 765 the Shias split over who should be the seventh Imam of the prophet Muhammad, following the death of Jafar al-Sadiq. The Ismailis claimed Jafar's late son Ismail. Founders of the North African Fatimid Empire, the now Nizari Ismailis have an uninterrupted leadership of Imams to the current Aga Khan. Since the 19C the heartland of the sect has been in India, where they are also known as Khojas.

Beliefs

The current Imam or Aga Khan guides the faithful. 'Belief in Allah' and to 'remain good citizens of their countries' is central. The Ismailis are Muslims who have an esoteric belief. The universe is a cyclic process with seven (not five as for many Muslims) pillars of faith: belief, purification, prayer, almsgiving, fasting, pilgrimage and struggle in Allah's way.

Points of interest

Fatimid Empire   Or Fatmid Caliphate from 909 to 1171 centred on Cairo (triumphant), Egypt and included the holy cities of Mecca, Medina and Jerusalem.

Assassins   The Nizari branch of the Ismali's were known by Christian crusaders as Hashishiyn, or hashish addicts, who carried out assassinations of their enemies. The word assassin is derived from the word Hashishiyn.

Racing colours   Green, red epaulettes and green cap.

Organisations   Aga Khan Development Network and Institute of Ismaili Studies.

Aga Khan   IVth Aga Khan and 49th Imam, Karim al-Husayn Shah, was born 13th December 1936 in Geneva. Educated at Le Rosey School, Switzerland and Harvard University, he succeeded his grandfather, Aga Khan III, as Hazar Imam (Living Leader), on 11th July 1957, aged 20.

HH   His Highness, title granted by Her Majesty the Queen in 1957.

Aga Khan   Title meaning Lord and Master.

Notably AWOL   Shergar the Wonderhorse, who in '81 won the Derby and in '83 was 'lost' in Ireland.

JAINISM

- Ascetic Philosophical Religion
- 6C BCE India, UK, USA & Africa
- Mahavira (Great hero)
- 5 million
- www.jainworld.com

HISTORY

Although followers see the faith as eternal and uncreated, the 'founder' Mahavira, who was the last of 24 Tithamkara's ('ford-makers') or perfected souls, discovered the ultimate truth for which he is venerated. Jainism, which is derived from Jina or 'conqueror' (of passions, attachments and aversions), split into two main sects in 79, the Svetamabaras or 'white clad' and Digambaras or 'sky clad' (naked).

BELIEFS

All things are inhabited by an immortal soul (Jiva), enmeshed in temporary matter (Ajiva). Nirvana, or salvation, is obtained by freeing the soul through purification and perfection. The fog or heavy Karma that precludes this is lifted by the Mahavrata (vows) of absolute non-violence, personal suffering, honesty, no stealing, chastity and non-possession.

POINTS OF INTEREST

Time Is an eternal cycle of descent and ascent. The decline is in six periods: mankind without care; diminution of bliss; appearance of sin; requirement for guidance; further decline (current period); live as animals. Then the ascent, in reverse order, to an Age of Gold.

Sallekhana Holy Death is the practice of fasting to death. The ultimate penance to work off bad Karma.

Nirvana Liberated souls attain bliss, for eternity.

Mahatma Ghandi's Non-violent civil disobedience views were influenced by Jainism.

Symbol The outline of the symbol represents the universe. The lower half is hell with the hand reminding us to stop and consider our actions, especially toward violence. The middle, or waist, is the earth. Above which are the heavens for the liberated souls who have the right faith, conduct and knowledge. The swastika represents the four 'arms' of life/reincarnation: heavenly, human, animal and hellish.

Insects Efforts are made to not harm any creature. Monks sweep the paths as they walk and wear masks to avoid any harm to insects.

JEDI

- Way of the Force
- 25,000BBY Galaxy-wide
- Yoda
- Unknown
- www.starwars.com

HISTORY

'A long time ago, in a Galaxy far away', in the city of Coruscant the Old Order of Jedi Knights was founded. The Jedi 'were the guardians of peace and justice in the Old Empire'. Subsequent civil wars divided the Jedi into the Light Side and Dark Side (Sith). Yoda the greatest Jedi Master was born in 896BBY. He trained Luke Skywalker who founded a New Order of Knights, many of whom now live on Earth.

BELIEFS

Governed by a Council of twelve Masters, the Jedi are 'unified by their belief and observance of the Force'. The Force is a natural mystical 'energy field created by all living things'. Adepts are, after complicated and graduated training, able to contact and harness the Light Side of the Force to considerably increase their perception and physical abilities.

POINTS OF INTEREST

BBY Before the Battle of Yanvin (Luke Skywalker v Death Star). A Galactic year is 368 days each of 24 hours.

Yoda 'Do or do not, there is no try'.

Lightsaber Sword like Jedi weapon invented in 9,990BBY. A concentration of the Force through crystals producing a beam or blade.

Ranks Padawan (apprentice), Youngling, Jedi Knight, Jedi Master and Jedi Spirit.

Sith An ancient brotherhood who, having learnt to use the Dark Side of the Force (evil), are the enemy of the light-sided Jedi.

George Lucas Author and variously director and producer of the Star Wars films.

Films The Phantom Menace ('99), Attack of the Clones ('02), Revenge of the Sith ('05), A New Hope ('77), Empire Strikes Back ('80) and The Return of the Jedi ('83).

Notable In the 2001 UK National Census 390,000 citizens returned Jedi Knight as their religion.

Hero with a Thousand Faces 1949 Joseph Campbell book and Star Wars inspiration. A Hero's journey, underpinning all myths.

'May the Force be with you'

JEHOVAH'S WITNESS

- Christian Unorthodox non-Trinitarian
- 1872 USA & worldwide
- Jehovah
- 6 million
- www.watchtower.org

History

The International Bible Students Association of Pittsburgh The Watchtower and Bible Tract Society was formed in 1872 by Charles Taze Russell, the first President, after a crisis of faith. The organisation in 1931, now under Joseph Rutherford, adopted the name Jehovah's Witness. The next President, Nathan Norr, started the school that trains missionaries (Publishers and Pioneers) and leaders (Elders and Overseers).

Beliefs

Jehovah is the one God. The Bible is the infallible literal text and true word, especially the Hebrew Scriptures (Old Testament). Jehovah created earth for his own purpose to become after Armageddon, (initially considered to be 1914) an earthly paradise (God's Kingdom) forever for the chosen living and resurrected dead. 'Millions now living will never die'.

Points of interest

Jehovah Biblical name for God. From Hebrew JHVH plus vowels.

Isaiah 'You are my witnesses' says the Lord 'and my servant whom I have chosen'.

Publications Monthly, for bible study and doctrine The Watchtower, which is the world's most widely read religious magazine, and Awake! for general interest. Both translated into c.148 languages to 80+ countries.

Blood Blood to mouth or veins violates God's laws (Leviticus). So no blood transfusions or indeed any stimulants whatsoever.

Unpopular World powers and political parties are allies of Satan. No military service, no saluting national flags, no pledges of allegiance.

Afterlife No hell or afterlife so extinction for those not chosen to join new Kingdom.

Christ Died on a stake not a cross.

Door to door Every centre (Kingdom Hall) sends its Publishers and Pioneers on door to door preaching.

Sometime Notables D Eisenhower (military leader), Venus and Serena Williams (tennis), Michael Jackson (at times) and the Artist Prince.

JESUITS

SEE CATHOLICISM & BENEDICTINE ORDER

- Roman Catholic Missionary Order
- 1534 Rome and worldwide
- Christian God
- 20,170
- www.sjweb.info

HISTORY

The Society of Jesus was founded by St Ignatius of Loyola at the time of the Catholic 'counter reformation' and received Papal licence in 1540. A disciplined order of male missionaries and teachers ('Schoolmasters of Europe'), their sole allegiance to the Pope led to unpopularity in Europe and subsequent suppression in 1773. Restored in 1814, Jesuits now operate over 450 schools and colleges in 112 countries.

BELIEFS

Based on three vows of poverty, chastity, and obedience especially and only to the Pope and no other hierarchy. St Ignatius's contemplations or 'Spiritual Exercises' underpin the Society's training, doctrines and prayers. In order to imitate Jesus Christ, the pious self-disciplined followers travel anywhere to propagate their faith. No dress code required.

POINTS OF INTEREST

Motto Ad Majorem Dei Gloriam or All things for the greater glory of God.

Spiritual Exercises Outline the relationship between God and man and the acceptance of the law of God.

Stoneyhurst College 1593 English Jesuit public school. Alumnae include Gerard Manley Hopkins (poet), Conan Doyle (author) and President George W Bush's great-great grandfather.

The Moon 35 lunar craters were named after Jesuits, by astronomer Riccioli.

Jesuitical A derogatory adjective meaning 'crafty'.

Black Pope The General Superior is alleged to be the world's most powerful man.

Gregorian Calendar In 1582 Jesuit Christopher Clavius, for Pope Gregory XIII, corrected Caesar's Julian calendar that was gaining time. October 5th to the 14th October were omitted.

Tonic 'Jesuits bark', or Quinine from the bark of the Cinchona tree, was brought to the West by the Jesuits. A tonic for all, bar mosquitoes.

General Superior Dutch Father Peter-Hans Kolvenbach in 1983 became the twenty-ninth Jesuit leader.

JESUS ARMY

- Christian Contemporary Evangelical
- 1973 UK
- Jesus Christ
- 2,600
- www.jesusarmy.org.uk

History

Noel Stanton, a Baptist Pastor of Bugbrooke Chapel, Northampton, was moved by the Holy Spirit in a charismatic experience to found the Jesus Army, Jesus Fellowship and New Christian Community in the 1970's. The Army is noted for their help and, some time, conversion of alcoholics, drug addicts and generally the less fortunate, its communal church households and its inner city 'friendship evangelism'.

Beliefs

Orthodox mainstream Christian beliefs include adherence to the Apostles, Nicene and Athanasian Creeds. In particular that Jesus is the Son of God and only via him can entry be sought to the Kingdom of God. Communal living and the belief in sharing, to the extent of giving all wealth to a 'common purse' and proactive campaigning are more radical.

Points of interest

Friendship Evangelism   High profile, peer-to-peer street evangelism or a form of viral marketing.

Glossolalia   The speaking in tongues which often accompanies baptism in the Holy Spirit. It is reported that the 'tongues' sometimes sound Middle Eastern.

Witness-wear   Logoed baseball caps, T-shirts and fleeces.

Church households   Include   Battlecentre (London),   Anchorage   (Birmingham), Abundant Grace (Coventry), Holy Treasure (Kettering), Lighthouse (Liverpool), Crown of Life (Sheffield).

House of Goodness Ltd. Trading arm with interests in farming, health food, retailing, builders' merchants, timber and engineering. £35 million turnover in 2003 includes Goodness Foods, Towcester Building Supplies, Skaino Amos, White and Bishop and Mason Bullock.

Bugbrooke Hall   Listed 1815 Old Rectory, now New Creation Hall.

Publications   Streetpaper and Jesus Life are two.

Transport Brightly coloured, sign written, double decker buses are used to visibly spread the word.

KABBALAH

SEE ORTHODOX & REFORM JUDAISM

- Jewish Esoteric Mysticism
- 12C Europe, Israel & USA
- Ein Sof, the Infinite and Limitless
- Unknown
- www.kabbalah.com

HISTORY

Born from the ancient Merkavah mysticism of Ezekiel and the chariot of fire ascending to heaven. Isaac Ben Abraham 'the Blind' (who first used the name) founded a scholarly movement in 12C France. The teachings spread to Spain where Moses de Lion is attributed with writing the Book of Splendour (Zohar), the faith's main text. From there it has spread to become a fashionable modern-day answer to life.

BELIEFS

Kabbalah means 'received' or 'what has been received' from God. God and mankind are bound together in a community of fate and destiny where every human action has an effect on heaven. The Zohar outlines the mystical contact points between mankind and God via the ten symbolic stages (Sefirot) as a map of consciousness, or tree of life.

POINTS OF INTEREST

Sefirot The emanation from, or qualities of, Ein Sof that link mankind to God are depicted as a tree of thirty-two paths. On the left (feminine aspect) are: Intelligence and Understanding; Power; Dignity. On the right (male aspect) are: Wisdom; Grace and Mercy; Eternity. Down the centre (the balance): Thought; Beauty; Foundation; Kingdom.

RE-INVENTION Name of Madonna's 2004 tour.

Zorah A commentary on the inner meaning of the five books of Moses (Torah); has been compared to a shelter for all things, or ark.

K2Oils Aromatherapy oils sold online by the Kabbalah Centre include Inspiration, Frankincense and Sensual. All contain Kabbalah water.

Three levels of the soul Nefesh is the lower unconscious or base animal instinct. Ruach is the middle soul, which distinguishes between good and evil. Neshamah is the upper soul that can never die.

Bracelets Wearing of a red thread/string bracelet is said to be an amulet to ward off the evil eye.

Notables Madonna, Demi Moore, Brittany Spears.

KIMBANGUISM

- **Christian Independent Church**
- **1921 Congo and central Africa**
- **Simon Kimbangu**
- **6.5 million**
- **www.kimbanguisme.net**

History

Kimbanguism is the largest Christian movement in Black Africa, whose adherents transcend class, tribal and national boundaries. In April 1921 Kimbangu, a Bakonga Baptist, began healing the sick and raising the dead. He was imprisoned for sedition for life by the Belgian colonial power only to become a Messianic figure. His Church received legal recognition in 1959.

Beliefs

The Church of Jesus Christ on Earth through the Prophet Simon Kimbangu, is a member of the World Council of Churches and practices a Christianity resulting from the actions and lessons of the prophet (ngunza) Simon Kimbangu. Additionally it believes that Kimbangu himself is 'Saint-Esprit' or God and part of the Christian Holy Trinity.

Points of interest

Kimbangu Simon (1887-1951) succeeded first by youngest son Joseph Diangienda (1918-92) and then by grandson Kiangani.

Kimbangu says 'The black will become white and the white black'.

Colours Green for hope and white for purity adorn all.

Bakongo Ethnic and original people of the 'Kongo'.

Bread and wine is substituted by sweet potato and honey. The Eucharist is given on only three days, 6th April (ministry began), 12th October (death) and 25 December (Christ's birth).

Nkamba The 'New Jerusalem' of the Low-Congo. Kimbangu's village of birth and also his gravesite.

Poles apart Or 'lat zero', the Equator which, in 24,092 miles, crosses only 13 countries including the Congo.

DROC Equatorial country, the Democratic Republic of Congo, aka Zaire and Belgian Congo.

Record 1999 Guinness Book of Record's World's fastest growing religion.

No Puritan views reject violence, polygamy, magic, witchcraft, alcohol, tobacco, dancing and eating primates.

LUTHERAN WORLD FEDERATION

- Christian Lutheran Protestant
- 1947 Germany, Europe & now worldwide
- Christian God
- 60 million
- www.lutheranworld.org

HISTORY

In the early 16C Martin Luther, the Father of the Protestant Reformation, attacked some of the more worldly practices of the Catholic Church. The result was an exodus from the Roman Church and military and political conflict. The Augsberg Peace of 1555 resulted in the maxim 'of whom the rule, of him the religion'. The 1947 Lutheran World Federation is the largest association of Lutheran Churches.

BELIEFS

The 1580 Book of Concord outlines Lutheran doctrines. The central tenets are: justified by faith alone (Sola Fide), by the grace of God rather than by actions (Sola Gratia), through the Bible (Sola Scriptura), by Christ (Sola Christus) and to the Glory of God (Soli Deo Gloria). Emphasis is on formal services, preaching and congregational singing.

POINTS OF INTEREST

Die Bible Luther was the first person to translate the Bible into German in the 1520's and 30's from the Greek Erasmus Bible.

Hymns Now Thank We All Our God and A Mighty Fortress Is Our God.

Diet of Worms Church meeting in eponymous city in 1521 concluded by declaring Luther an outlaw.

Countries 15 with over one million Lutherans each. Including Germany, Denmark, Norway and Finland.

Bach Johann Sebastian, Lutheran composer of Mass in B minor and the Brandenburg Concertos.

No relation Martin Luther 'I have a dream' 'beyond Vietnam' King, the black equal rights campaigner and 1964 Nobel Peace Prize winner.

31ˢᵗ October 204th day of the year and Reformation Day. The day in 1517 that Luther nailed his theses.

Martin Luther German monk and religious reformer 1483-1546. His 95 theses, a protest against Catholicism, were famously nailed to the door of Wittenberg Castle Church.

Notable Baywatch's David Hasselhoff, 'TV's most watched star'.

METHODIST WORLD COUNCIL

- Christian Anglican Evangelical
- 1720's UK, USA & worldwide
- Christian God
- 60 million
- www.worldmethodistcouncil.org

History

The World Methodist Council is the umbrella organisation for the Methodist Church in Britain and the USA-based United Methodist Church, which is the largest. John Wesley, after a 'strangely warmed' religious experience, founded Methodism in the 1720's. A now 'methodical' global presence has seen and survived separation from and failed reintegration's with the Church of England and many internal schisms.

Beliefs

'Revealed in Scripture, illumined by tradition, vivified by personal experience and confirmed by reason'. Christian Protestant orthodoxy, with a methodical pursuit of biblical and personal holiness together with Christian perfection. In particular a belief that all need saving, all can be saved, all can be assured of salvation and all can be saved completely.

Points of interest

Strangely warmed John Wesley (1703-91), an Anglican priest, member of Oxford's Holy Club and travelling evangelist on 24th May 1738 had his faith renewed while attending a meeting in Aldersgate, London.

Covenant Service Annual renewal of faith with God.

Hierarchy Church in Circuit in District in Conference in Council in Connexion.

Hymns Loud and fast and ever popular. 6,000+ written by Charles Wesley (brother), including O for a Thousand Tongues to Sing and the carol Hark the Herald Angels Sing.

Cross and Flame Notable symbol of the United Methodists of the USA. The cross for Christ and the everlasting flame of the Holy Spirit.

Methodist Recorder Newspaper founded in 1861, motto 'the truth in love'. 1993 story that Preachers to wear uniform and be trained in clowning and juggling was the paper's first April fool.

UN First ever meeting held in Westminster Methodist Central Hall, London in 1946.

US Presidents Polk (11th), Grant (18th), Hayes (19th), McKinley (25th) and G 'W' Bush (43rd).

MORMONS/LATTER DAY SAINTS

- Christian Evangelical
- 1830 USA & worldwide
- Christian God
- 11 million
- www.lds.org

History

God and Jesus Christ visited Joseph Smith Jnr, first in 1820. He was then visited in 1822 by an angel (Moroni), who led him to two gold plates bearing the teachings of the Apostle Mormon, which are the word of God. Smith translated them into The Book of Mormon (1830). Initially persecuted the Mormons were forced West from New York to found Salt Lake City, in what is now Utah, from whence they have grown.

Beliefs

Christianity died with the death of the last Apostle until restored by Smith. The Book of Mormon, Doctrines and Covenants and Pearls of Great Price together with the parts of the Bible that are translated correctly outline the faith. Continual revelation of God, baptism, repentance and the eternal family lead to the attainment of the Celestial Kingdom.

Points of interest

Baptism of the dead Allows proxy baptism for those who have died without having heard the Gospel, thus giving them the chance to be saved.

TV Mormon Philo T Farmsworth, aged 14, was one of the most important inventors of the television.

Mountain Meadows An alleged massacre by the Mormons in 1837 of 137 pioneers, who had surrendered.

Word of wisdom God gave a law of health which directed no tobacco, alcohol, coffee, tea or illegal drugs.

Eternal families Marriages last even beyond death.

Brigham Young Smith's successor who founded Salt Lake City and became the first Governor of Utah had 20 wives and 47 children.

Tithing Every Mormon contributes 10% of their income to the Church.

Mormons in the majority In Arizona, California, Idaho, Nevada, Oregon, Utah, Washington and Wyoming they have more congregations than any other church.

Polygamy Or Polygyny was accepted until The Great Accommodation in 1890.

Notables Gladys Knight, The Osmonds (singers).

NATION OF ISLAM

SEE SUNNI, SHIA, ISMAILI, SUFISM AND WAHHABI

- Unorthodox Black Muslims
- 1930 USA, Canada & UK
- Allah & Wallace D Fard
- 25-100,000
- www.noi.org

HISTORY

In 1930 the Nation of Islam or the Lost Found Nation of Islam in the Wilderness of North America was founded by Master Wallace D Fard, a self-proclaimed Mahdi, to unite the Asiatics of America. Fard disappeared in 1934 and his mantle was taken by Prophet Elijiah Muhammad. After Muhammad's death in 1975, Louis Farrakhan took control of a movement diminished by the desertion of adherents to mainstream Islam.

BELIEFS

Allah, Muhammad, the Koran and Islam is the faith of the Asiatics of the Shabazz tribe, who are the blacks of America and Allah's chosen and righteous people. Specific 'wants' include freedom, justice, reparation for slavery in the form of an independent state, release of all Muslims held in prison, no racial intermarriage and exemption from tax for all blacks.

POINTS OF INTEREST

Asiatics Or Moors of Morocco are the ancestors of all black Americans. A theory first expounded by Noble Drew Ali, founder of the Moorish Science Temple of America in 1913.

Shabazz Tribe of 'those of direct African descent and earth's original people'.

Malcolm X Or Malcolm Little or El-Hajj Malik el Shabbazz. Spokesman for the Nation and cultural 'by any means necessary' hero of the 1960's. Later disaffected and assassinated in 1965.

X Represents pre-slavery lost African tribal name.

Louis Farrakhan Born Louis Eugene Walcott, later Louis X, author of the 1950's calypso song 'White Man's Heaven is Black Man's Hell'.

Million 'black' Man March To Washington DC in 1995. Farrakhan's showpiece.

Prescient 1 'Chickens coming home to roost'. Malcolm X's quote about President 'JFK' Kennedy's assassination on 22nd November 1963.

Prescient 2 UK Home Secretaries who have refused Farrakhan entry to Britain are Hurd, Straw and Blunkett.

Mahdi Expected Messiah of the Muslims, a hidden Imam.

NATIVE AMERICAN CHURCH

- Peyotism or Pan-Indian Peyote Church
- 1918 USA & Canada
- Great Spirit
- 250,000
- www.nativeamericanchurch.com

History

Since time immemorial it is believed that the indigenous Mexican peoples (Toltecs and Aztecs) venerated the 'Divine plant', Peyote. In the 19C its use spread to the Reservations of the Southern American Plains tribes including the Huichols, Kiowa, Comanche, Apache and Navajo. In 1918 the Native American Church was formed to try and avoid prohibition and protect religious freedoms. Opposition continues.

Beliefs

The hallucinogenic Peyote is seen variously as a sacramental substance with holy powers, a healing medicine, a means of communication with the Great Spirit God, and a deity by itself. Two schools, Quanah Parker's Half Moon Way and the Big Moon or Cross Fire Way incorporate to a lesser and greater extent some Christian symbolism in their ceremonies.

Points of interest

Peyote Or *Lophophora Williamsii* is a spineless cactus, which takes up to thirty years to flower, and is increasingly endangered. Its crown or button contains mescaline and is dried and chewed or drunk boiled in water. From the Nahuatl word meaning silk cocoon.

Mescaline Psychedelic drug which acts on the central nervous system causing introspection, euphoria, insight, intense colours and sounds leading to an altered state of consciousness.

Roadman Shamanistic ceremonial leader of the Peyote Way or Road.

Ceremonies Normally monthly on a Saturday night in a tipi with the door facing East. Around the fire the ritualised smoking, singing, taking of Peyote, drinking water and prayer take place. Ends with breakfast.

Legendary The Teachings of Don Juan by Carlos Castaneda. University of California Press 1968. 'An extraordinary spiritual and psychological document'.

Quanah Parker Last Chief of the Comanche, political and religious leader who is quoted as saying 'follow after white way, get education, know work, make living'.

OPUS DEI

See Catholicism (Roman)

- Conservative Catholic 'Work'
- 1928   Spain, Italy & worldwide
- Christian God
- 85,000
- www.opusdei.org

History

In 1928 Spaniard Josemaria Escriva founded the influential lay conservative, and sometime controversial, organisation Opus Dei (God's Work) or what is now The Priestly Society of the Holy Cross. Escriva published his seminal book The Way in 1939 and word of the 'Work' was spread. He died in 1975 and was beatified in 2002 by Pope John Paul II who had already made Opus Dei a Personal Prelature of the Vatican.

Beliefs

Orthodox strict Catholicism, where the laity 'spread throughout society a profound aware-ness of the universal call to holiness'. A belief that everyday life, its customary activities and, in particular, ordinary work should lead to holiness, personal Christian perfection and God. Prayer, sacrifice and humility are central to its influential and secret membership.

Points of interest

The Way Four million copies in 43 languages of the 999 short maxims of Escriva. An easy reading masterpiece.

Waypoint No 1 'Don't let your life be barren. Be useful. Make yourself felt. Shine forth with the torch of your faith and your love'.

Donkey 'Oh blessed perseverance of the donkey.' Escriva handed out model donkeys instead of photographs.

June 26 Feast day for 'the Saint of the Ordinary' Escriva who died on this day

Fishing Or a method of recruitment into residences of holy discretion.

Cilice Optional spiked metal leg band. A constant thorn in the side, as it were.

Heroic minute A mortification of will is to rise immediately upon waking.

Ranks Celibate resident Numerary, celibate Associate, lay active Super-numerary and Co-operator.

Nicknames Unkindly as The Holy Mafia, Octopus Dei and the Saints and Schemers.

Dei wear Atkinsons' Cologne is said to be favoured.

Mortification 'Let us bless pain, love pain, sanctify pain … glorify pain'.

ORTHODOX EASTERN CHURCH

SEE RUSSIAN ORTHODOX CHURCH

- Christian Religion
- 1C E & SE Europe and worldwide
- Christian God
- 140 million
- www.ec-patr.gr

HISTORY

The Eastern Orthodox communion of autocephalous churches is the living continuation of the Church of the Apostles of Christ Jesus. Constantinople became the New Rome of the Roman Byzantine Empire, which split from Old Rome's Catholic Church in the Great Schism of 1054. The Patriarch of Constantinople is the first among equals or honorary leader of all other Patriarchs, of which the Russian Church is the largest.

BELIEFS

The 'Apostolic faith once delivered to the Saints has been preserved inviolate' as defined by seven ecumenical councils. Belief of: God the Father the creator as eternal and first of the Holy Trinity; Christ Jesus incarnate as man and God; Holy Spirit and Virgin Mary (Theotokos). Mysteries (sacraments), prayer, icons, fasting and almsgiving are key.

POINTS OF INTEREST

Septuagint Bible Or LXX, is a 4C Greek translation and variation of the Hebrew Old Testament plus Apocrypha. The Orthodoxies' orthodox.

Icons Sacred images, often of Christ, the Holy Mother and Saints are 'windows into Heaven'. The representation only is worshipped.

Feast and famine Ten immovable and two movable great feast days of 'joyful exhaustion'. Offset by no meat, fish etc. fasts of the Great Fast (Lent), the Apostles, Dormition, pre-Christmas and Wednesdays and Fridays.

Christmas day 7th January.

Patriarchs The ancient sees of Constantinople, Alexandria, Antioch and Jerusalem, plus six national and other independent Churches.

St Andrew Founder of the Church of Constantinople. Patron Saint of Greece, Scotland and single women.

Bartholomew I Or Dimitrios Arhondonis, since 2nd November 2002 the 270th Patriarch of Constantinople.

Istanbul Was Constantinople until 1930. The Turkish 'city' astride the Bosphorous, in Europe and Asia.

Autocephalous Federation of independent churches.

ORTHODOX JUDAISM

See Reform Judaism & Kabbalah

- Classical Monotheistic Religion
- 19C Israel & worldwide
- Jewish G-d
- 2 million
- No single seminary

History

A descendent of the original Rabbinic Judaism of +2,000BCE, which believes that G-d instructed Abraham (first Jew), to leave Egypt and settle in Canaan. In 70 the Romans destroyed the Temple/city of Jerusalem and the Jews fled forming into two main European traditions, the Sephardic (Spanish) and Ashkenazi (German). It is from the latter that the modern Orthodox movement sprung in the 19C.

Beliefs

G-d's literal written law (Torah) and immutable verbal law (Talmud) was told to the prophet Moses. It is thus of divine origin, representing the covenant between G-d and Israel. The other principal beliefs are the one all knowing eternal G-d is the creator, has no form, and rewards good and punishes bad. A Messiah will come and the dead will be resurrected.

Points of interest

Talmud The law code containing the six Mishnahs on Agriculture, Appointed Times, Women, Damages, Holy Things and Purity, together with an explanation.

Kashrut Permitted (Kosher) food includes no meat and dairy together; only meat from a cud-chewing cloven hoofed animal, fish that have fins and scales.

Get A bill of divorce, which, if signed, allows a wife to remarry upon divorce. 'No Get, no remarry'.

Dress code Skull cap (Kippa), wool and linen not mixed. Black coats.

Torah First five Books of Moses (Old Testament); Genesis, Exodus, Leviticus, Numbers and Deuteronomy.

Matrilineal Orthodox Jews are descended through the female line.

Ark of Covenant Acacia wood box containing the Ten Commandments and the Talmud. Lost in 586BCE when the Babylonians destroyed the first Temple of Jerusalem.

Circumcision Eight days after birth. Compulsory.

Orthodox From Greek, 'straight' and orthos, 'opinion'.

PEOPLES' TEMPLE

- Jonestown Christian suicide sect
- 1950's USA & Guyana
- Jim Jones
- Survivors disbanded
- www.jonestown.sdsu.edu

History

The Peoples' Temple was founded in Indianapolis by James Warren Jones in 1955 as the Wings of Deliverance. A member of the Christian church (Disciples of Christ), it grew from its base in Ukiah, California to include a Temple in San Francisco. In 1974 Jones opened the Peoples' Temple Agricultural Mission in Guyana where, on 18th November 1978, 'revolutionary suicide' killed 914 and ended the mission.

Beliefs

The rainbow family of 'Dad' Jones had a self-styled theology or Cause. Initially based on elements of Christian Pentecostalism, the doctrines and theories developed into a form of 'God Almighty Socialism' or 'Apostolic Socialism'; a just society would always overcome the evils of racism and poverty that were so prevalent in capitalist USA.

Points of interest

Revolutionary suicide Or murder-suicide by poisoning, took 276 children and 638 adults, by order of Jones.

Memorial Every year at Oakland's Evergreen Cemetery where 408 unclaimed members are buried.

'Drinking the Cool Aid' Purple coloured Flavor Aid or Cool Aid laced with cyanide, valium, penegram and chloral hydrate was the cocktail of choice. Dry runs had been rehearsed as 'White Night' loyalty tests.

Conspiracy theory Q875 Jonestown: a mind control experiment of the CIA.

Guyana Third smallest South American country, after Suriname and Uruguay, that gained independence from Britain in 1966.

Jonestown 3,852 acres of jungle in the Orinoco river basin, leased by the Guyana government to the Peoples' Temple 'to cultivate and beneficially occupy'.

Snake Dance Notable book by survivor L Kahalas unravels the mysteries of why.

US Congressman Leo Ryan Murdered on the day of the suicides by cult members while visiting Jonestown on behalf of concerned relatives.

PURE LAND BUDDHISM/AMIDISM

SEE THERAVADA, ZEN, & TIBETAN BUDDHISM

- Devotional Mahayana Tradition
- 2C BCE Japan/China & the West
- Amitabha or Amida
- Over 25 million
- www.2.hongwanji.or.jp

HISTORY

After the death of the Buddha, two main schools of Buddhism developed in India; Mahayana and Theravada. Mahayana spread into China and Japan where it developed into Pure Land or Amidism. In 1175 Honen founded the Jodo Shu School (Shu) and then in 1214 his disciple Shinran founded the Jodo Shin-shu School (Shin). These are today the largest Pure Land Buddhist Schools, with Shin the bigger.

BELIEFS

The beliefs of Amidism are centered on the veneration of the Amida Buddha. Pure Land or Western Paradise is a concept that allows the faithful, who are unable in life to achieve true Buddhist enlightenment or Nirvana, to be reborn or progress, after death to Sukhavati. Having the wisdom of absolute faith in Amida attains this 'Easy Path'.

POINTS OF INTEREST

Practices The main practices include meditation, worship and chanting of Amida's name (nembutsu), together with the offering of prayers and presents to him.

Nenju/Juzu Buddhist rosary beads used as a prayer aid.

Pure Land sutras The three scriptures are the Small, the Large and the Discourse on Meditation. They cover Amida's vows and the origins and nature of the Pure Land.

Obutsudan Home altar normally containing an image of Amida, together with flowers, incense and food offerings, often rice.

Amida Monk Dharmakara later Buddha Amitabha or Amida (of limitless light or life) vowed to save mankind. He created the Pure Land.

Shoko Incense burning is a spiritual act, which cleanses and brings to mind the transience of life.

Nembutsu Reciting 'Namu Amida Butsu' earns merit.

Sukhavati Amida's Pure Land or Western Paradise, which is in the western quarter of the Universe. A land of happiness, utmost bliss, free of sickness and suffering and, most importantly, a one-way ticket to true enlightenment.

QUAKERS/FRIENDS
SEE SHAKERS

- Christian Non-conformist
- 1652 Chiefly UK, USA & Kenya
- Christian God
- 400,000
- www.quakers.org

A Quaker meeting can be... Would you like to share it with us?

HISTORY

The Religious Society of Friends was founded in England by George Fox in 1652. Fox's proclamation "tremble at the word of the Lord" earned the name 'Quakers'. Robert Barclay in 1676 wrote Apology for the true Christian Divinity, which became the statement of doctrine. Persecuted in England in the 17C William Penn (founder of Pennsylvania) and others emigrated to the USA. A schism in 1827 resulted in four main sets.

BELIEFS

The 'Religion of the Inner Light', a true religion which refuses to be defined by creed or dogma. Instead concentrating on a personal relationship of individual worth with Jesus and guidance of the Holy Spirit. Friends relate with the risen Lord without priests, rituals, services, and sacraments. Firmly committed to pacifism, equality, doing good and moral purity.

POINTS OF INTEREST

Peacemaker The Peace Testimony believes that the indwelling light of God precludes any taking up of arms.

Chocolate Quaker Joseph Fry is credited with making the first chocolate bar. George Cadbury and Joseph Rowntree were also Quakers.

Originally Quaker Barclays Bank, Wedgewood, Reckitt, Bryant and May, Price Waterhouse, JW Thompson.

Sets From the original Hicksites, Guerneyites, Orthodox and Wilburites there are now Friends General Conference, Friends United Meeting and Evangelical Friends Int.

Bible Was written by man acting under the Holy Spirit and is therefore not the final revelation of God.

Worship 'A visitor to a Quaker meeting stands up after five minutes of silence and asks, "When does the service begin?" An old Friend rises and after a brief reflection says, "Service begins when the worship ends".' (Anonymous).

Marriage Is the work of the Lord and not for the priest/magistrate.

Notables H Hoover and R Nixon (31 & 37 USA President), James Dean (actor).

RASTAFARIANISM

- Messianic Religio-Political
- 1930 Jamaica & elsewhere
- Haile Selassie I
- 1 million
- www.rastafarian.net

History

In the 1920's, Jamaican Marcus Mosiah Garvey, of the Back to Africa Movement (UNIA), predicted the 'crowning of a black prince he shall be the redeemer'. So when in 1930 Prince Ras Tafari was crowned Haile Selassie I (power of the Trinity) of Ethiopia the religion was born in Jamaica. Rastafari has today developed into a diverse organisation, from the original anti-white movement.

Beliefs

Beliefs include: Haile Selassie as the living God (Jah), repatriation to Ethiopa/Africa (the promised land Zion), liberation from Babylon (whites/Jamaica). Black supremacy as the true Israelites of the Bible, reparation for historic wrongs (slavery). Of late, self-help, love and peace and the liberation of Jamaica are included.

Points of interest

Flag Crowned Lion of Judah on Ethiopian flag. Green = Ethiopian land, Red = blood of martyrs, Gold = wealth.

Marijuana/ganja The wisdomweed or sacramental herb is smoked in worship. 'Herb for the service of man', Psalms 103:14.

Food Strictly organic vegetarian (I-tal). At worst no scavengers e.g. pork, lobster, crab.

Sets House of Nyabinghi, Bobo Shanti, 12 Tribes of Israel.

I and I The concept of oneness, man with Jah and everyone, Jah is all.

Texts Kebra Negast (Glory of Kings), Fetta Negast, The Bible, The Holy Piby (Black mans' Bible).

Festivals Haile Selassie's birth 17th August, coronation 2nd November, Jamaican visit (Grounation) 21st April. Freedom 1st August.

Some Bob Marley albums Exodus, Songs of freedom, Babylon by bus, Dreams of freedom, Rastaman vibration.

Dreadlocks Unwashed, unbrushed, uncut hair equates to rebellion. A Lion's mane.

Notables Leonard Howell (first preacher), Bob Marley and Peter Tosh (singers).

REFORM JUDAISM

SEE ORTHODOX JUDAISM & KABBALAH

- Modern enlightened Judaism
- 1800's Europe & USA
- Jewish God
- 3.75 million
- www.rj.org

HISTORY

Jews in Germany during the early 1800's started to question the ancient laws and teachings of Orthodox Judaism. During the Age of Enlightenment (Haskalah), Rabbis Abraham Geiger and Samuel Holdheim, philosopher Moses Mendelssohn and others felt that Judaism should be progressive and adaptable to the modern world. Reform Judaism sees itself more as a union/community of Jews, than a nation of Israel.

BELIEFS

Liberal Judaism is a progressive faith that has modified some rules of the interpretive Orthodoxy. Less ritualistic, it concentrates on equality, inclusiveness, repairing the world and social justice. While affirming a living God, his laws (albeit as an ongoing revelation) and Israel, the Reform does so with freedom and choice.

POINTS OF INTEREST

Calendar Starts from the creation of the world in 3,761BCE. Jewish year is either deficient (353 days), regular (354) or complete (355) and broadly starts in September. Each month starts with the new moon.

Gay/lesbian Controversially allowed full participation.

Shabbat Sabbath is 25 hours out of time from Friday night. Less strictly observed today.

Zionism The nationalistic movement to restore Israel to the Jews is now supported by the Reform, although the tenet that all those living elsewhere are in exile is not.

Women The Reform believes in the total equality of women including female rabbis and allows mixed seating in synagogues.

Yiddish Language of the Jews, a German dialect influenced by Hebrew.

2005 Jewish year 5765/6.

Notable Jewish surnames Einstein, Goldblum, Abramovich, Spielberg, Rothschild, Kafka, Houdini, Bernstein, Wiesenthal and Geller.

Yom Hashoah Holocaust remembrance day, 18th April. Often includes the lighting of six candles to signify the six million dead.

RUSSIAN ORTHODOX CHURCH

See Orthodox Eastern Church

- Orthodox Christian
- 988 Russia & worldwide
- Christian God
- 90 million
- www.mospat.ru

History

The distinct faith of Russia was born with the baptism of Prince Vladimir of Kiev in 988. The Church grew rapidly in the years that followed, climaxing in the 15C when Moscow proclaimed itself the Third Rome. The Patriarchy has since suffered swings in fortune. Abolished by Tzar Peter I in 1727, re-established in 1917, oppressed by the Communists, influential in WWII and since the 1991 fall of the Soviet Union enjoying greater religious liberty.

Beliefs

'The life of the Church is a life in communion with God himself, in the truth and love of Christ, by the Holy Spirit'. The seven Holy Mysteries (sacraments) are central: triple immersed child Baptism, Chrismation (confirmation), 'sacramental change' of the Eucharist's bread and wine, three Orders, confessional Penance, Marriage and Anointing of the sick.

Points of interest

Moscow Patriarchate   Is the fifth in honour of all Patriarchies and was established in 1589. The current (just) and 15th Patriarch is 1929 Estonian born Alexey Mikhailovich Ridiger, now more simply, Alexy II.

Trinity Icon   By greatest medieval icon master and monk, Andrei Rublev.

Iconostasis   The icon wall which separates nave and sanctuary, or spirit and flesh, in Orthodox churches.

Domes   A feature of the churches are the dome shaped roofs. The original being Hagia Sophia.

WWII   Church funded the St Dimitry Donskoy Tank Column and the St Alexander Nevsky Squadron for Stalin.

Chrism   Holy oil.   12lbs of myrrh and cassia, 6lbs of cinnamon and cane, plus herbs and one gallon of olive oil.

Tsars   Include a Fake, False, Blessed, Terrible and Great, before Emperor Nicholas II in 1918, the Bloody Unlucky?

Russian Cross   Top bar is Pontius Pilate's inscription plate reading 'Jesus of Nazareth, King of the Jews'. The middle bar is where Christ's hands were nailed. The bottom bar is the footrest.

SALVATION ARMY

- Conservative Evangelical Christian
- 1865 UK & worldwide
- Christian God
- 1.5 million
- www.salvationarmy.org

HISTORY

(General) William Booth founded the Whitechapel Christian Mission in 1865, which in 1878 changed its name to The Salvation Army, in order to perform social work and 'save the derelict' in London's East end. The Army, whose motto is 'Heart to God and hand to man', continued to grow under the second General Booth (Bramwell). Today, under General Larsson, it operates in 109 countries and 175 languages.

BELIEFS

Centred on its Articles of War which enshrine eleven beliefs: scriptures constitute divine rule, one perfect God, Jesus Christ also God, all mankind depraved as a result of fall from innocence of Adam and Eve, Jesus' atonement allows salvation provided there is repentance, justified by grace, obedient faith, all believers sanctified and immortality of the soul.

POINTS OF INTEREST

International Staff Band Founded by Bramwell Booth in 1891 to 'deny the devil the best tunes' the brass band now has a repertoire of 994 hymns and 251 choruses.

War Cry! The Army's monthly magazine founded in 1879. 'Ever as our war cry, victory!' Booth.

USA's most popular charity In 1995 raised $742 million.

Cab Horse Charter Booth's original mission was for the poor to have nightly shelter, food and work just as the London cab horse did.

Pop music 1964 chart top 20 with 'It's an open secret'.

Uniform The wearing of the red/black uniform represents: commitment to war versus evil, personal testament to faith and availability.

Abstinence From alcohol, tobacco, drugs, gambling, pornography and the occult.

Structure International headquarters London, then Territories, Divisions, Corps and Citadels (churches).

Doughnuts In WWI France Salvationist Helen Purviance invented the 'doughboy' to feed US troops. Still sold in USA at Fred Meyer and Ralph's stores, the unique ingredient being nutmeg.

SATANISM/CHURCH OF SATAN
RELIGION OF THE LEFT-HAND PATH

- 1966 USA, UK & elsewhere
- Satan
- Secretive
- www.churchofsatan.com

HISTORY

Satanism has existed in some form since the ancient Egyptian God of Chaos and Evil (Set), via the 17C European Satanic cults and 18C aristocratic Hell-Fire clubs of England. Religious Satanism and the Church of Satan was formed in San Francisco by Anton LaVey in 1966, now run by a Blanche Barton. In 1975 Satanist Michael Aquino founded The Temple of Set which is the main rival in a discordant seminary.

BELIEFS

Man is a carnal beast with hedonistic urges and appetites. The main Satanic beliefs are: indulgence over abstinence; actual existence over spiritual dreams; wisdom over self-deceit; vengeance rather than turning 'the other cheek'; sin leads to mental, physical, and emotional gratification, responsibility to the responsible and not to 'psychic' vampires.

POINTS OF INTEREST

Satanic Bible LaVey's 1969 thesis that outlines custom and practice and has been translated into Danish, Spanish and Swedish. ISBN: 03800015390, not 666. Also by LaVey, The Satanic Witch and Satanic Rituals.

Left-hand Path In modern occultism the phrase generally means individual advancement of self and free thought over all else. Derived from the Bible's Book of Matthew 25.33 sheep to the right, goats left.

Rituals Allegedly three forms, sexual (gratification), compassionate (charitable) and destructive (to others).

Baphomet Originally a deity of the 12C Knights Templar. The modern symbol is of a circle with a goat or ram's face inside a point down or inverted pentagram.

Congregations Collectively known as grottos, pylons or temples.

Metals Gold is a Christian metal, so silver preferred.

AKA Lucifer, Old Nick, Set, Devil, Beelzebub, Al-Shaytan, Samael, Dark Lord, Infernal Majesty and Prince of Darkness amongst others.

Black Mass Parody of the Catholic mass with a naked woman's back as the altar.

SELF REALIZATION FELLOWSHIP

- Kriya Yoga & Meditation
- 1920 The West & India
- Yogananda
- 'Hundreds of thousands'
- www.yogananda-srf.org

History

Western Yoga has evolved from the pre-history shamans of Asia, via the Vedic and Hindu scriptures and the classical yoga of Patanjali's 2BCE Yoga-Sutras. Paramahansa Yogananda was one of the first yogis to bring the teachings from India to the West. He formed the Self Realization Fellowship in 1920, which has grown from its Los Angeles headquarters to include 500 plus meditation centres worldwide.

Beliefs

'We are all part of the One Spirit. When you experience the true meaning of religion, which is to know God, you will realise that He is your Self, and that He exists equally and impartially in all things'. The spiritual harmony and principles of truth from both Hinduism and Christianity can, through the graduated exercises of Kriya Yoga, lead to the soul's liberation.

Points of interest

Strap line 'Fellowship with God through Self-realization, and friendship with all truth-seeking souls'.

Autobiography of a Yogi The 1946 best selling modern spiritual classic, 'A Journey through Life's Lessons.' ISBN No: 0876120796.

Yogoda Satsanga The Indian sister organisation founded in 1917, now based in the city of Ranchi.

Mahasamadhi A God realised Soul's final conscious exit from the body at will. Yogananda's did so in March 1952 and his mortal body did not decay at all for 20 days.

Patanjali The first man to record the ancient practice of Yoga. He describes an eight-fold path of moral conduct, observances, posture, control of life force (prana), withdrawal, concentration, meditation and subconscious experience.

Yogic paths Royal Raja, physical Hatha, devotional Bhakti, wise Jnana, selfless Karma and mystical Tantra.

Kriya Yoga A complete system of techniques for blissfully realising God and Self.

Yoga A yoking union of spiritual, or more commonly physical, disciplines.

SEVENTH DAY ADVENTIST

See Branch Davidians

SEVENTH-DAY
ADVENTIST
CHURCH

- Christian Faith Community
- 1863 USA & worldwide
- Christian God
- 14 million
- www.adventist.org

HISTORY

William Miller, of the Millerites, predicted the second coming/advent of Jesus Christ as 22nd October 1844. After the 'great disappointment' Joseph Bates, James White and Ellen G White (who had a vision of an angel) claimed that Miller was wrong and that October 1844 was actually the start of a new era of judgement. The movement has grown from its home in Maryland, USA to more than 90% of the world's countries.

BELIEFS

In most respects, Adventists are traditional Christians who believe that the Bible is the written word of God, and that mankind is free to chose a path. They are, however, differentiated by the view that the second coming is imminent, delayed only by the failure to proclaim the Gospel to all and by the lack of observance of the Sabbath.

POINTS OF INTEREST

Second coming   Will be actual and visible to all. After which 1,000 years for the good in Heaven, while Satan inhabits a desolate earth. Thereafter a 'second resurrection' to a cleansed earth.

Pitcairn Island Seventh Day Adventist is the main religion for the 50 or so inhabitants of the British South Pacific island.

Era of Judgement An investigative period of judgement and the cleaning of the heavenly sanctuary before the Second Advent. When the living and dead are assessed for their readiness to enter God's Kingdom.

Logo Bible is the base, over which is the open word of God with the cross in the centre.   The burning flame of truth is above.

Hospitals The church runs over 600.

Cornflakes and Rice Krispies John Harvey an Adventist, founded Kellogg's, the now $9 billion company.

Sabbath   Seventh day of the creation of the world by God was a Saturday.

Radio Adventist World Radio covers 70% of the world's population. Available in Europe via the Internet or the Satellite Hotbird 6.

SHAIVISM

See Hinduism, Vaishnavism & ISKCON

- Major Hindu denomination
- 3,000BCE S & W India, Kashmir
- Shiva or Siva
- 280 million
- www.shaivam.org

History

The Shaivites are reputedly the oldest continuing sect of the complex amalgam that is the Hindu faith of the Indian subcontinent. The stone age Indus civilisation worshipped 'an agricultural and pastoral fertility god' Rudra, who is considered the forerunner of Shiva. Shaivite theology developed into a number of diverse forms, Trika (Kashmir), Pasupata (Gujarat), Saiva Siddhanta and Lingayats (Tamil South).

Beliefs

Ascetic, meditative and yogic. Shaivites are part of the Hindu Dharma so believe that the soul, whose ultimate aim is liberation, is part of a constant cycle of death and rebirth over many lifetimes, with each incarnation subject to previous actions. Central to liberation is the worship of and adherence to the immanent and transcendent God, Shiva.

Points of interest

Shiva Lord of yoga, dance and animals, the creator, preserver and destroyer. Shiva is often portrayed as a four armed ash covered dancer in the centre of a ring of fire that represents a periodic destruction of the universe.

Ash The Tilak mark of the Shaivites is three lines of ash on the forehead. Ash is symbolic of the end; as in ashes to ashes, dust to dust.

Matted hair Of Shiva and his adherents symbolises the ascetic, as well as the source of the River Ganges.

Nandi Holy milk-white bull that is Shiva's vehicle.

Shivarati Principal festival in February/March.

Mt. Kailash 22,000ft Himalayan mountain in Tibet, with darshan (divine views) on a clear day. Shiva and his partner Goddess Parvati's home.

Linga Is a phallus or 'wand', inserted in a base which represents the female genitalia (Yoni). Shiva's symbol of fertility and 'creative energy'.

Great sex The Kama Sutra or love God Kami's 'manual'. First translated by linguist Sir Richard Burton in 1883. ISBN No: 0972269169, with illustrations.

Mantra Om Namah Shivaya.

SHAKERS

SEE QUAKERS

- Communal Millenarian Christian
- 1740's England then USA
- Dual God, both male and female
- www.shaker.lib.me.us

HISTORY

From a branch of the Quakers, the 'Shaking Quakers' (later the United Society of Believers) emerged. 'Mother' Ann Lee, of Manchester, UK experienced a series of divine revelations and in 1774 left for America with eight others. Under J Meacham and L Wright the Society prospered. By the 1840's there were 6,000 followers in 19 'villages'. The only one that remains is Sabbathday Lake in Maine.

BELIEFS

'Mother' Ann Lee, who to some was the second coming of Christ, believed the source of human sinfulness was sexual intercourse. In order to live a life of perfection it was necessary to withdraw from the sinful World and dedicate to celibacy, hard work and religion. The 'villages' believed in a community of goods, pacifism and ritualistic dancing/shaking.

POINTS OF INTEREST

Mother Lee "Hands to work, hearts to God".

Dancing The ecstatic ritual practices of dancing, whirling and singing were influenced by the Protestant Camisards of Cevennes, France.

Guinness Book of Records States it is the World's smallest sect.

Celibacy Single beds in single sex dormitories only.

Songs Some 12,000 songs written. None more famous than 'Simple Gifts' by Elder Brackett. It has provided the melody to Lord of the Dance and Appalachian Spring.

Inventions Shakers are credited for the commercial oven, rotary harrow, circular saw, flat head broom, screw propeller and apple corer.

Shaker Your Plate Shaker cookbook by Sister Frances A Carr is still available.

Building rules No fanciful decorations, meeting houses are white outside and a blueish shade inside. Barns red, workshops ochre.

Furniture Form followed function. Simple and symmetrical, from mostly pine.

Notable The ladder back, slat-back or 'common' chair. Originals up to £15,000.

SHIA IMAMIS

SEE SUNNI, ISMAILI, SUFI, WAHHABI, NATION OF ISLAM

- Shia Islam
- 622 Iran, Iraq, Pakistan & India
- Allah
- 80 million
- www.khamenei.ir

HISTORY

The Ithna Ashari, Imamis or Twelvers are the largest sect of Shia Muslims who, after the death of the Prophet Muhammad in 632, claimed Muhammad's cousin and son in law, Ali ibn Abu Talib, as legitimate successor and not the other three Caliphs of the Sunnis. Ali was followed by 11 related Imams (successors) the 12th of whom, the Mahdi, disappeared in 939. Shia Islam is now the state religion of Iran.

BELIEFS

'There is no God but Allah, Muhammad is the messenger of God, Ali is the friend of God'. The Imamis are part of the Muslim community (Umma) and mainly share similar beliefs to all Muslims. However, there are differences over the infallibility and suffering of the Imamate, interpretation of the Koran and law (Sharia), practices and authority of the clergy.

POINTS OF INTEREST

Shia Shiat Ali or Party of Ali.

Ali c.600-661, the second or third ever convert to Islam. Married to the 'perfect woman' Fatima and father of Husayn and Hassan. Murdered and buried near Najaf.

Najaf Shia pilgrimage sites to the graves of Ali, Adam and Noah, in Iraq.

Husayn Third Imam, martyred on 10th October 680 at the Battle of Karbala, Iraq. His mausoleum there is an important pilgrimage site.

Ashura Holy day of 10th October to remember Husayn. Includes lamentation, mourning and self-mutilation.

Prayer Three times a day, prostrate with grounded forehead after light feet washing.

Taqiyya Permitted dissimulation (concealment of one's faith) to avoid persecution. Uniquely Shia.

Khomeni Ayatollah and Paris based leader of the 1979 Iranian Revolution.

Khamenei One of five living Ayatollahs and Supreme Leader and Chief of State of the Islamic Republic of Iran.

al-Mahdi The 12th and awaited or hidden Imam, Muhammad Muntazar, will emerge at the end of time.

SHINTO

- 'This Worldly' Way of the Kami
- Formally since 6C Japan
- Kami
- 100 million shrine members
- www.jinjahoncho.or.jp

HISTORY

An unstructured mix of nature worship, fertility cults, divination techniques, hero worship and shamanism of the indigenous Japanese that was only named Shinto in the 6C, upon the arrival of Buddhism. Shinto co-existed with other incomer religions until in 1868 Emperor Meiji made it the only official state religion under a programme of National Learning; in 1945 after World War II religious freedoms were reinstated.

BELIEFS

The will of the Japanese people, personified by conventions that precede or transcend religion, which focus on an optimistic 'simple and harmonious life with nature and people'. Devotion and communication with invisible spiritual 'omnipresent manifestations of the sacred' beings (Kami) who are able to maintain harmony and beneficially intervene in life.

POINTS OF INTEREST

Kami Vast myriads of heavenly and earthly Kami include creator, ancestor, nature and guardian Kami that are worshipped in shrines.

Kamikaze Or Divine Wind.

Four affirmations Tradition and the family, Love of Nature, Physical cleanliness and Matsuri (the Kami festivals).

Ema A small tablet or offering (and substitute for a horse) for making wishes to the relevant shrine's Kami.

Myth and legend Recorded in the 8C books of Kojiki (Records of Ancient Matters) and Nihongi (Chronicles of Japan).

Torii The gateway or portal into a Shinto shrine. Generally made of two posts supporting two lintels.

Amaterasu The chief Kami, a Sun Goddess and ancestor deity of the imperial family. Her shrine at Ise, which is rebuilt every 20 years, was that of State Shinto.

Ginkgo The Maidenhair tree, a living fossil with no relatives, its leaf shape is the official symbol of Tokyo.

Subsets There are/were Shrine, Sect, Imperial, State and Folk forms of Shinto. Shrine Shinto has c.100,000 shrines across Japan.

SIKHISM

- Monotheistic Religion
- 1499 Punjab in NW India & UK
- Ek Onkar
- 20 million
- www.sikh.org

History

Guru Nanak, the first of ten gurus, founded the Religion of the Gurus or Sikhism in 1499. The last of the human gurus was Guru Gobind Singh (1675-1708) who initiated the soldier saints of the Khalsa and decreed that his successor was to be the sacred scripture of the Adi Granth. The Sikh panth (path) has continued to fight for its corner of India, Punjab, with variously the Mogul, British and Indian administrations.

Beliefs

'A Sikh is any woman or man whose faith consists of belief in one God, in the ten Gurus, and the teachings of the Guru Granth Sahib and the ten Gurus and who has faith in the amrit of the tenth master and who professes no other religion'. A third way of bhakti devotion between Hinduism and Islam with few rituals or impediments to truthful living.

Points of interest

Translation A guru is the teacher of a Sikh, who is the learner or disciple in a panth or path of sweet ambrosial undying amrit.

Adi Granth The noble first book and definitive text is known as the Guru Granth Sahib, and is the embodiment of the gurus as well as being the 11th guru itself.

5k's The code of discipline for pure Khalsa men includes the requirement to wear: Kesh (uncut hair and beard), Kangha (comb), Kripan (sword), Kach (shorts) and Kara (bangle). All men are named Singh (Lion) and all women Kaur (Princess).

Amritsar Or pool of nectar, is Punjab's largest and holiest city and home of 5th Guru Arjan's Golden Temple or Hari Mandir.

Beginning of the end British rule in India after the 1919 Amritsar Massacre of 380 civilians by British soldiers; Indira Ghandi's life after the storming of the Golden Temple in 1984.

Khalistan 'Muslims got Pakistan, the Hindus got India, what did the Sikhs get?'

Punjab The land of five rivers whose capital Chandigarh was designed by architect Le Corbusier in the 1950's.

SOKA GAKKAI

- Value Creating Nichiren Buddhist
- 1930's Japan and now worldwide
- 12 million
- www.sgi.org

History

Soka Gakkai is a lay Buddhist organisation that was started in the 1930's by Makiguchi Tsunesaburo and Josei Toda. Since World War II the Society has become the most successful Japanese new religious movement. Under Ikeda Daisaku since 1958, it has split with its 'parent' Nichiren Shoshu, involved itself in Japanese politics, courted controversy, become a United Nations NGO and spread to 190 countries.

Beliefs

A belief that 'every individual has the potential to become enlightened in his or her present lifetime' and so reach Buddhahood. Through a personal revolution and reformation involving faith, practice and study, everyone can attain happiness and success and so by definition can society as a whole. The ultimate aim being a beautiful and good world.

Points of interest

Nichiren Or Sun Lotus, a 13C Buddhist monk who maintained that the Lotus Sutra held the 'key to transforming people's suffering and enabling society to flourish'. He established the sacred title (daimoku) 'namu myoho renge kyo' meaning 'I take refuge in the Lotus of the Wonderful Law Sutra.

Lotus Sutra The Buddha's c.2C Lotus of the True Law.

Gohonzon A mandala scroll or diagram of 33 Sanskrit characters around the daimoku that is 'the prime point of faith, practice and study'. The 1279 original is in the Taisekjii Temple in Japan.

Shakubuku Literally to 'break and subdue' until converted. An oft criticised recruitment policy.

New Komeito The New Clean Government Party. Japan's third largest political party on a Soka Gakkai ticket of 'humanitarian socialism'.

White Lotus Nelumbo nucifera, sacred water lily that flowers and fruits simultaneously. Petals for wine, flowers for syphilis.

Ikeda Daisaku Son of a seaweed harvester who at 32 become the third President. Variously 'a statesman, billionaire and God'.

SPIRITUALIST NATIONAL UNION

- Religion of Spiritualism or Reason
- 1848 USA & now worldwide
- The Departed
- Unknown
- www.snu.org.uk

HISTORY

Spiritualism, as opposed to the ancients' ancestor worship and divination, is credited to Swedish scientist Emanuel Swedenborg in 1744 and, after his departure, to Medium Andrew Jackson Davis. Modern Spiritualism and public interest started in 1848 New York with the Fox sisters and their rappings. A Mrs Hayden in 1852 was the first Medium in England. Millions now accept Spiritualism in some form.

BELIEFS

'At death, the personality of an individual is transferred to another plane of existence with which communication from the world of the living is possible'. The seven principles are infinite Fatherhood of God, unselfish Brotherhood of Man, Communion of Spirits, eternal Human Soul that can Progress, Personal Responsibility and judgement of deeds.

POINTS OF INTEREST

Spirit The essential part of man that survives death.

Medium Person who is the channel between the departed and living. Mediumship takes two forms: Physical where the spirit raps; speaks or appears; or Mental where the Spirit communicates via the Medium's mind.

Also including Trances, séances prophecy, clairvoyance, healings and writings.

AJ Davis The 'John the Baptist' of Spiritualism, or Ploughkeepsie Seer, who wrote The Principles of Nature (1847) and The Harmonial Man (1853).

Hydesville rappings Kate and Margaretta Fox communicated with murdered pedlar Charles B Rosna, via audible raps, a sort of unmusical Morse Code.

Sherlock Holmes Arthur Conan Doyle is President-in-Spirit of the Spiritualist National Union; last words were 'You are wonderful'.

Houdini Magician and sceptic, before his death on 31st October 1926 vowed to communicate from the grave, if possible. No word so far.

Anagram Emanuel Swedenborg becomes 'Angel rowed sunbeam'.

SUFISM/TASAWWUF

SEE SUNNI, SHIA, ISMAILI, WAHHABI, NATION OF ISLAM

- Islamic Mysticism
- 8C Asia, Africa and now the West
- Allah
- Unknown
- www.ias.org

HISTORY

Sufism is an umbrella term for a collection of diverse spiritual Islamic Orders, which started with 8C anti-worldly ascetics, like al-Hasan and Rabia of Basra. Many brotherhoods, influenced by the martyr 'I am the Truth' al-Hallaj and the Persian philosopher 'revelation over reasoning' al-Ghazali were organised in the 12C. Often persecuted by puritan 'orthodox' Muslims, the 1960's saw the New Age West take interest.

BELIEFS

The Sufi Way, substantiated by the Prophet Muhammad's actions and Koranic passages, is to seek 'close, direct and personal experience of God' through love and, '... dedication to worship, total dedication to Allah most High, disregard for the finery and ornament of the world, abstinence from the pleasure, wealth and prestige sought by most men'.

POINTS OF INTEREST

Sufi Believed to derive from the Persian for garments of coarse wool often worn.

Tariqa The path or way, a concept of being.

Mystical Path Via repentance, abstinence, renunciation, poverty, patience, trust in God and satisfaction.

Dhikr Ritual observance and remembrance, often with dancing. Whirling Dervishes or Mevlevi are a Turkish Sufi Order.

Intoxicated and sober Types or states of Sufi brotherhood, the former drunk with the spirit of God, in an exalted state, the latter not.

Idries Shah Author of The Sufis (1964) and The Way of the Sufi (1968), helped bring Sufi mysticism to the West.

Enneagram Nine sided mystical diagram lately used as a personality tool, attributed by some to George Gurdjieff and the Sufi's. The nine points are reformer, helper, achiever, individualist, investigator, loyalist, enthusiast, challenger and peacemaker.

Walis Friends or Sufi saints.

Notable Omar Khayyam (Tentmaker) the 11C Persian author of the Rubaiyat of four lined verses first translated in 1859 by Edward Fitzgerald.

SUNNI MUSLIM

See Shia, Ismaili, Sufi, Wahhabi, Nation of Islam

- Majority Islam
- 622 Middle East & worldwide
- Allah
- 1 billion

History

The Prophet Muhammad was the last and therefore 'Seal' of the biblical prophets who recorded Allah's word, received from the Angel Gabriel (Jibril), in the Koran (Quoran). Sunni's are the traditional mainstream 'people of the path' of Muhammad's successors, the four Caliphs. Sunni is the largest (c.90%) grouping within Islam, which is the world's fastest growing religion. Mecca (Makkah) is the focal point for all.

Beliefs

'In the name of Allah, the Merciful, the Compassionate'. There is one just God whose word is the Koran, which together with the prophethood of Muhammad and his Hadith, constitute the tradition (Sunnah) of the orthodox Sunni. There is also a belief in: prophets, angels and a final Day of Resurrection and Judgement, with an afterlife. Inshallah.

Points of interest

Islam Means peace and submission to Allah.

Muslim Means one who submits to Allah.

Pillars of Islam The five are: profession that 'no god but Allah' (Shahada), five daily prayers (Salat), annual alms giving (Zakat), fasting during daylight hours of the ninth month (Ramadan or Sawm) and pilgrimage to Mecca once in every lifetime (Hajj).

Other prophets Abraham, Noah, Moses and Jesus.

Hadith Collection of sayings and doings of Muhammad, which are an important part of the Islamic law, Sharia.

Koran Meaning recitation, is the divine revelation and greatest sign of Allah. 114 chapters (suras) each divided into verses (ayats).

Caliphs Muhammad's four successors were Abu Bakr, Umar (who founded the city of Basra in 636), Uthman and Ali (Muhammad's cousin and first Imam of the Shia).

Muhammad's maulid Or birthday is 12 Rabi al-Awaal, the third month.

99 Whoever knows the Koran's 99 divine names of God will go to Paradise. The 100th name of God is hidden and known only to the camels.

TAOISM

SEE CONFUCIANISM & ZEN BUDDHISM

- Religion of the Divine Way
- 6BCE China & Taiwan
- 20-30 million
- www.taorestore.org

HISTORY

As with Confucianism, the start of Taoism is rooted in the nature worship, shamans and divination of the ancients. It is believed that philosophical Taoism was started by Lao Tze in the 6CBCE, developed by Chuang Tzu and became the state religion of China in c.440BCE. Whilst never a unified code, Taoism's Way has permeated every aspect of Chinese culture, although 20C restrictions have reduced that influence.

BELIEFS

The unnamed and infinite Tao or Way is the primordial source and principle order in, and unity of, the Universe. A lifetime search for and attempt to become one with the Way will lead to physical immortality. All things, if left alone, have a natural course, flow and harmony but Gods, rituals, superstitions, alchemy, health and hedonism all came to play a part.

POINTS OF INTEREST

Tao-te-Chin The Book of the Way and its Power, or way, virtue and energy. A 5,000 character book allegedly written in three days by Lao Tze (Old Man or Master) that can be read in 'half an hour or a lifetime'.

Immortals Perfect men or spiritual beings that 'dine on the air and sip the dew'. A heavenly host.

Three jewels Compassionate kindness, moderate sincerity and humility.

Wu Wei Active inactivity. Water flows downhill 'it works without working'. 'The way to do, is to be'.

Five elements From Yin and Yang: fire, water, earth, wood and metal.

Tai Chi Chuan Exercises of body and mind that through the centring of chi (the life spirit, a breath of air) and with 'an investment in loss' lead to 'effortless action'.

Beware 'He who stands on tiptoe doesn't stand firm. He who rushes ahead doesn't go far. He who tries to shine dims his own light'.

Yin Yang Two pandas, or the symbol of balanced complementary opposites. A soft healing female yin and a masculine hot hard yang.

THE FAMILY

- International Christian Fellowship
- 1968 100+ Homes worldwide
- Christian God
- 12,000
- www.thefamily.org

History

An often controversial organisation that has variously been called the Children of God, Teens for Christ and the Family of Love. Founded in 1968 by 'Father David' or 'Moses David' (Dad) Berg in Huntington Beach, California to make a difference for the 'lost generation of the hippie counter-culture youth'. Since Berg's death in 1994 his wife, Karen or Maria, reportedly continues to head the Family from hiding.

Beliefs

The modern day evangelical Christian and humanitarian fellowship claims to be far removed from the high demand doomsday millennial free love anti-system control cult that it is accused of having been. Although still proclaiming an imminent 'Great Tribulation' and the second coming of Jesus, the mission now is to 'comfort, aid and minister to those in need'.

Points of interest

Love Charter 1994 constitution outlining the Family's rights and responsibilities.

Ffers Or 'Flirty Fishing'. A recruitment campaign, which ended in 1987 and involved enticing new members through sex or the suggestion of. Also known as 'hookers for Jesus'.

Berg 'The devil hates sex but God loves it'.

Endtime prophets David and Maria or Karen Zerby.

Family music Mp3 downloads include 'Children of the Sun' 'I Trust U' 'No Matter What' 'If You Give Love' and 'Break Away'.

FREECOG Free our Children from the Children of God was formed in 1971 as one of the first ever anti-cult organisations. The American Family Foundation, at www.csj.org, is currently the most influential.

MO letters The writings of David Berg circulated to the membership. Titles include 'The Lover of all Lovers' and 'Little People'.

Notable Actor River Phoenix of My Own Private Idaho fame who died, aged 23, of a drug overdose outside the Viper Rooms in Los Angeles in 1993 was raised in part by the Children of God.

THERAVADA BUDDHISM

See Zen, Tibetan & Pure Land Buddhism

- Southern Orthodox Original Tradition
- 480BCE Sri Lanka & SE Asia
- Buddha, the supreme teacher
- 124 million
- www.accesstoinsight.com

History

Siddharta Gautama an Indian prince, having witnessed sickness, aging, death and the peace of a monk, left his family to search for an end to suffering. Under a Bodhi tree he received full insight and was thus enlightened (Buddha). After his death (c.480BCE) his disciples met to write down his teachings in the Tripitaka. Theravada (the way of the elders) is the earliest and truest interpretation. Continues to spread.

Beliefs

To reach the state of an Arhat it is necessary for believers to enlighten themselves by literally following the Buddha's own example, insight and teachings (Dharma). This means accepting the universal and noble truths, following the eightfold path and five precepts. Self-effort, wisdom, alms giving, meditation and pilgrimage comprise the path to Nirvana.

Points of interest

Four truths Everything is impermanent and suffers; craving or desire results from suffering; suppress craving to eliminate suffering; follow the eightfold path.

Eightfold path The spokes of the Dharma wheel represent the right speech, action, livelihood, effort, mindfulness, concentration, view and resolve.

Arhat Saint or 'worthy one' who has achieved Nirvana and thus escaped the endless cycle of death and re-birth.

Bodhi tree Ficus religiosa or Bo tree Fig is the tree of Wisdom. Original in Bihar, India.

Tripitaka Or Pali Canon is the text of the 'three baskets' that outline the faith's doctrine. Divided into the Vinaya Pitaka (rules for the Sangha (monks and nuns)); the Sutta Pitaka (central teachings or Suttas) and Abhidhamma Pitaka (logic).

Precepts The five are: no killing, no stealing, no sexual misconduct, no lies and no intoxicants.

Puja Monastic gatherings for meditation and reverence.

Gordon Douglas First Westerner to be ordained to the Sangha (monkhood) in 1899 in Myanmar/Burma.

TIBETAN BUDDHISM

See Theravada, Zen & Pure Land Buddhism

- Northern Vajrayana Tradition
- 7C Tibet, Mongolia & the West
- Dalai Lama
- 10 million
- www.tibet.com

History

An esoteric mix of compassionate Bodhisattva Mahayanan and mystical Tantric Buddhism, incorporating the indigenous shamanistic folk religion of Bon, developed in Tibet via a series of 'diffusions'. The four major schools are the Nyingma (Ancient ones), Sakya (Grey earth), Kagyu (Oral lineage) and Gelu (Way of virtue), which is led by the Dalai Lama, who has been in exile since the 1950's Chinese invasion.

Beliefs

The path to enlightenment (Nirvana) is attained by following the Buddha's teachings (Dharma) and in particular those of the Bodhisattva of Compassion, Avalokitesvara. Followers of the Vajrayana or 'diamond way' use a guru/lama as guide to the many Gods, spirits, practices, rituals, ceremonies, symbols and mantras, so that Nirvana can be hastened.

Points of interest

Sunlight City Lhasa, Tibet's capital at 3,658m (12,000ft) is the world's highest city.

China Since the Chinese invasion and occupation many of Tibet's 6,000 monasteries have been damaged or destroyed.

Lama/guru Spiritual scholastic yogic teacher.

Lung Ta Prayer flags or 'wind-horses' are flown to transmit prayers. Five colours: blue (space), white (water), red (fire), green (wind), yellow (earth).

Mantra Sacred chant. Om Mani Padme Hum or Hail the Jewel in the Lotus is famous.

Prizes The Nobel Peace Prize was awarded to HH The Dalai Lama in 1989.

Notable Films *Seven Years in Tibet* and *Kundun*.

Biography Freedom in Exile, ISBN: 0060987014.

Llamo Dhondrub Birth name of Tenzin Gyatso (Ocean of Wisdom) or His Holiness (HH) the 14th Dalai Lama who, aged two, was recognised as the earthly manifestation of Avalokitesvara. Lama since 1940 and Head of State since 1950, he was forced into exile to Dharmasala (Little Lhasa), India, in 1959.

TRANSCENDENTAL MEDITATION

- Meditative Philosophy/Religion
- 1957 India and mainly the West
- 'Maharishi' Mahesh Yogi
- 5 million claimed
- www.tm.org

History

Descended from the ancient Hindu Vedic traditions as taught by Guru Dev whose pupil, Maharishi, founded the Spiritual Regeneration Movement in 1957 to spread the 'scientific' technique of Transcendental Meditation. In 1972 a World Plan was conceived to spread the Science of Consciousness to all and in 1976 a World Government for the Age of Enlightenment or Natural Law was created. The programmes continue.

Beliefs

Properly prescribed, twice a day for twenty minutes, creative meditation will 'release mental and physical stress' thus improving the potential of mind, body, behaviour and environment leading to enlightenment and the transcending of consciousness. Meditation takes the form of silent repetition of Sanskrit mantras or words, as directed by a teacher.

Points of interest

Yogic flying For the advanced 'meditator' the TM-Sidhi programme offers levitational hovering and in some instances forward hopping, while in a state of 'exhilaration, lightness and bliss'.

RAAM World Peace Bond or the Global Development currency, fixed at one RAAM to 10 Euro, is in limited use in Holland and elsewhere.

Maharishi Vedic City 1,100 acre city Near Fairfield, Iowa.

Beatles 'Jai guru deva om' a lyric from the 1970 song Across the Universe which has been translated as 'long live Guru Dev'.

World Plan One centre for every million people and one teacher for every thousand.

Natural Law Party A political party of 'conflict free politics and problem free government', which contested US Presidential and UK General elections. In 2000 it transcended into the Global Country of World Peace.

Maharishi book Science of Being and Art of Living. ISBN: 0452011426.

Notables David Lynch and Sir John Harvey-Jones, together with UK contact, Norma, tel 08705 143733.

UNIFICATION CHURCH (MOONIES)

- Ultra Conservative Evangelical
- 1954 Korea, USA & elsewhere
- Christian God
- 3 million
- www.unification.org

Welcome to
The Unification Church

The Holy Spirit Association for the Unification of World Christianity

---

History

On Easter Day 1935 Sun Myang Moon was charged by Jesus to complete his unfinished work. In 1945 Moon published the Divine Principle that outlines his teachings, a combination of Christianity and Confucianism. In 1954 Moon started The Holy Spirit Association for the Unification of World Christianity, sometimes referred to as The Moonies. Married in 1960 to Hak Ja Lan they became the Church's True Parents.

Beliefs

The world was created by God and represents a dual expression of life: Internal/masculine (Sung Sang) and External/feminine (Hyung Sang). The fall of man was represented by Eve having a spiritual relationship with Lucifer and then a sexual one with Adam. Jesus failed God's plan for the restoration of man by not marrying. Moon is the Messiah.

Points of interest

Mass weddings Of up to 40,000 at one time. Partners often chosen by the Moons as the True Parents are inter-religious, inter-racial, and cross cultural, representing the unity of mankind.

Media The organisation controls: Washington Times, News World, Insight, Middle East Times, Segye Llbo, Sekai Nippo and others.

Controversy Allegations of brain washing and deception coupled with financial indiscretions (Moon jailed for tax evasion in 1980's).

Crown of Glory Title of poem by Moon, aged 16.

Sinless children Any child borne to a mass wedded couple is free of original sin.

Seasonal days True God's Day, True Parent's Day, True Day of All Things, Declaration Day of God's Eternal Blessing, Foundation Day for Unified World.

Sets Professor's World Peace Academy, Conference on the Unity of Sciences, and International Federation for World Peace and many more.

Communism 'save mankind from the evils of ...'

Notables Three Moon children, Bill Gertz (author), Bo Hi Pak (right hand man).

UNITARIAN UNIVERSALIST

See Humanist

- Living Religious Humanism
- 1961 Mainly USA & Europe
- 'Reverence for life' or 'the Holy'
- 500,000 and expanding
- www.uua.org

History

'A non creedal, non doctrinal religion which affirms the individual's freedom of belief' result-ing from the 1961 union of the Unitarians and Universalists in Boston, USA, which is now broadly humanist. The Unitarians were descended from the 16C Christian 'non-Trinitarians' of Transylvania and Poland, via 17C England and J Priestley. The Universalists of Christian 'universal salvation' fame originated in 18C England.

Beliefs

A liberal, tolerant and inclusive organisation that has no required beliefs. Its independent congregations 'covenant, affirm and promote' a set of Principles and Purposes that stress the equality, worth and dignity of all and the respect of individual beliefs. Truth, world peace, liberty and justice are found from human experience and personal spiritual growth.

Points of interest

God A commonly held view is that the term God 'may appropriately be used as a name for some natural processes within the Universe, such as love or creative evolution'.

Joseph Priestley 1733-1804 English chemist who discovered dephlogisticated 'good' air or oxygen and founded the first Unitarian Church in America in 1796.

Ceremonies Water communion, Flower communion and Coming of Age.

Flaming Chalice Universally recognised symbol that unites the membership and symbolises the spirit of work.

Elevator speeches 'What's a Unitarian Universalist?' Answers to be given in the time it takes to descend six floors.

Adage 'The god of the cannibals will be a cannibal, of the crusaders a crusader, and of the merchants a merchant', by Ralph Waldo Emerson, Unitarian and essayist.

Superman The late Christopher Reeve, actor and founder of the Christopher Reeve Paralysis Foundation.

Servetus The father of Unitarianism, a 16C theologian and author of De Trinitatis Erroribus or the Erroneous Understanding of the Trinity.

VAISHNAVISM

See Hinduism, Shaivism & ISKCON

- Largest Hindu denomination
- 6-5C BCE Indian subcontinent
- Vishnu or Visnu
- 580 million
- www.vaishnava.com

History

Vaishnavism, in its various forms, is the worship of the transcendent, supreme, immanent and accessible God Vishnu. Originally a sun god, Vishnu's popularity grew in the post Vedic period (100BCE-400), with the Mahabharata and Ramayan poems. He and his emanations are the major deities of the reported 330 million continuing and connected gods of the disunited yet rich system of beliefs, which is Hinduism.

Beliefs

Devotion (Bhakti) to Vishnu and his chief incarnations Rama and Krishna order the life, principles and practice of all his adherents. Less ascetic than other branches of Hinduism, Vaishnavism still shares many of their rituals, traditions and lesser gods and especially the desire to escape the cycle of birth and death, as a consequence of action (Samsara).

Points of interest

Tilak Chandan or sandalwood mark to the forehead in the shape of a 'U'.

Rama Hero of the poem Ramayana, incarnation and now a common mantra.

Swaminarayan 18C Hindu movement who built the first European Mandir (temple) in Neasden, London.

Festivals Of hundreds, Diwali, festival of light (Oct).

Kali-Yuga The Age of Quarrel or Iron is the last of four ages (yugas) of the world. It started in 3,102BC and is 'scheduled' to last 432,000 years. The end is therefore not yet quite nigh.

Avatars The 9 emanations of Vishnu sent to earth from heaven (Vaikuntha) were: fish, tortoise, boar, man-lion, dwarf, Rama with axe, Rama, Krishna and Buddha. The 10th, Kalkin, a mighty warrior, is yet to descend.

Garuda Sun bird, serpent killer and Vishnu's transport.

Sri Lakshmi Vishnu's wife and lotus Goddess of wealth, good fortune and beauty.

Holy Basil Or Tulasi plant, a matchless herb and holy.

Vishnu The all pervading four armed periodic preserver and restorer of Hindu Dharma.

VOODOO

- Afro-Caribbean Folk Religion
- 18C Especially Haiti and Benin
- Bondye
- Who knows?
- www.vodoun.com

History

Haitian Voodoo is a direct descendent of the folk religions and snake cults of the Fon-Ewe, Yoruba and other peoples of West Africa. Slaves brought to French Haiti in the 18C maintained their traditional beliefs while incorporating a 'veneer' of Catholicism. In 1996 Benin, formerly Dahomey, accepted a form of Voodoo as an official religion and in 2003 the Haitian Government sanctioned Voodoo's existence.

Beliefs

A single 'High God' Bondye is supported by a pantheon of many nations/families of spirit gods (lwa/loa/Loa), including those of the ancestors, who control all worldly events. Rituals, sacrifices, dances and gifts are made to contact the relevant spirits in order to pacify them, or through possession by them to receive healing, good luck and advice.

Points of interest

Bondye From the French Bon Dieu or Good God.

Zombie Either the dead who have returned to a soulless life, or a dancer possessed by a spirit in trance.

Independence From France for Haiti in 1804.

Hougans and Mambos Priests and priestesses.

Veve Symbols drawn in the ground with powder to invoke certain lwas.

Related Santeria, (Cuba and S America), Obeah (Jamaica), Candomble (Brazil), Yoruba (W Africa) and Hoodoo (USA).

lwa groups Happy Rados of ancient Africa, angry Petro deities of the new world and Ghedes, the black dressed undertakers of the dead.

Voodoo Chile Legendary 1968 single by ex US paratrooper Jimi Hendrix.

Sacrificial lamb Or goat, or chicken, or dog. The possessed dancer to appease the spirits may drink blood.

Dolls Curses on individuals involving the sticking of pins into dolls is largely a Hollywood creation.

Variations on a theme Vudu, Vodun, Vodou, Voudoun and Vodum.

WAHHABI/MUTAWWIN

SEE SUNNI, SHIA, ISMAILI, SUFI, NATION OF ISLAM

- Conservative Sunni Islam
- 18C Mainly Saudi Arabia
- Allah
- Maybe 13 million
- www.saudinf.com

HISTORY

A Sunni Muslim movement founded on the Arabian Peninsular in the 18C by Ibn Abd al-Wahhab is viewed by its adherents as a restoration of true Islam, after Medieval deviations. Wahhab, who had been influenced by the orthodox Sunni Hanabili School, forged links with Muhammad Ibn Saud of the Saud family.   The still pro Wahhabi Saud family continue to rule the present day Kingdom of Saudi Arabia.

BELIEFS

A literal interpretation of the Koran (Quoran) with a return of strict adherence to traditional Islamic law. A reassertion of monotheism in the form of the Tawhid (unity and uniqueness of Allah). Denouncement and rejection of all Medieval practices such as shrine cults, Sufism, saint worship and other practices. A war (jihad) against non-conformers.

POINTS OF INTEREST

Kitab al-Tawhid Book by Wahhab that contains guidance on acceptable and unacceptable doctrine.

Bida Literally meaning innovation, is now synonymous with heresy. Amongst other things which are bida are alcohol, tobacco, some women's rights and western visitors to Mecca and Medina.

Mutawwa Religious police.

Halal Permissible and lawful food only, especially meat. Animals must be slaughtered by having their throats cut with a single swipe, while conscious. No blood or 'flesh of swine'.

Flag Green flag of Islam with ibn Saud's sword and inscription meaning There is no God but God; and Muhammad is his Messanger.

OPEC Organisation of Petroleum Producing Countries formed by Iran, Iraq, Kuwait, Saudi Arabia and Venezuela.

Saudi Oil 9 billion barrels per day (2004 est).

Mecca Holiest City, now in Saudi Arabia, birthplace of Muhammad and home of the Kaba: the structure at the centre of the world to which all prayers are directed (Quibla) and two million annually make pilgrimage.

WICCA OR WITCHCRAFT

See Druidry

- Pagan Nature based Religion
- 1950's Europe and N America
- The Mother Goddess & Horned God
- Thousands of covens
- www.wicca.com

History

The Old Religion or Craft, an unbroken (to some) pre-Christian tradition that survived the witch-hunts of early Europe. In the UK, after the 1951 repeal of the Witchcraft Act, Gerald Gardner and Doreen Valiente promoted 'Wicca' as a religion. Today Gardnerian Wicca ('low church'), Alexandrian Wicca ('high church') and Dianic Wicca (feminist) are the major branches, along with the traditional and hereditary.

Beliefs

Central to many of the disparate groups are the Wiccan Rede of 'An it harm none, do what thou wilt' and the consequence of any deed will return three times (Threefold Law). Worship of gods, in particular a female goddess who is 'maiden, mother and crone', reverence of nature, natural magic, high magic/magick, solar/lunar cycles and rituals.

Points of interest

Hedgewitch A cunning or wise solitary witch, with innate often hereditary powers who specialises in 'green arts, herbal cures and spells'.

Book of Shadows Or Grimoire is the witch's book of spells and rituals. Many Wiccans see Gardner's book as the defining text.

Halloween 31st October.

Tools of craft Athame (black handled magic sword), besom broom (sweeping circle and flight?), hazel wand (magic energy), cup, pentacle (symbol) and cauldron (e.g. for 'eye of newt and toe of frog' etc).

Pentagram A Wiccan ritual, five pointed star or endless knot. The points representing earth, air, fire, wind and spirit.

Gatherings Sabbats (on eight seasonal festivals) and Esbats (lunar rituals).

Great rite Or Sacred Marriage. Sexual intercourse between High Priestess and Priest either performed symbolically or for real, sometimes as part of the Drawing Down the Moon ritual.

Text of sort Culpepper's 1652 book Herbal. A cure all.

Wicca From Old English meaning to bend or shape.

ZEN BUDDHISM
See Theravada, Tibetan, Pure Land Buddhism

- Meditative Philosophical Religion
- 6C China, Japan & the West
- Bodhidharma
- Maybe over 10 million
- www.iriz.hanazono.ac.jp

History

Ch'an Buddhism was introduced to China in 6C by an Indian Monk, Bodhidharma. In the 12C Eisai, the founder of the Rinzai School, favoured by the aristocratic Samurai, brought it to Japan, as Zen. In the 13C Dogen created a second school, the Soto. Soyen Shaku and Suzuki introduced Zen to the West in the early 20C, where it flourishes as a vehicle for both students and intellectuals.

Beliefs

Bodhidharma said that Zen is a 'Special translation outside the Scriptures; not dependent on words or letters; pointing directly to the human mind; seeing into one's nature'. These higher and subtler teachings are attained by meditation (zazen), problem/riddle solving (Koan) and the direction of a master (sanzen/dokusan), leading to truth and enlightenment.

Points of interest

Flower sermon Or the Buddha's Silent sermon. A lotus flower was held in front of the disciples. Only one smiled and understood and so was handed the bloom, with the words 'what can be said, I have said to you. What cannot be said, I have given to Kasyapa'. Deeply Zen.

Ch'an/Zen From Dhyana, Sanskrit meaning meditation.

UNESCO World heritage site, the peaceful minimalist Zen garden of Ryoanji Temple, Kyoto has fifteen rocks in a sea of raked white gravel.

Grasshopper What is the sound of one hand clapping?

Enso Logo The circle of enlightenment, a symbol of 'no-thing', an infinity or void.

Lotus position Seated meditation, with each foot on the opposite thigh, like a giant pine tree. (Needs practice!)

Tea in China Bodhidharma during meditation cut off his eyelids in order to stay awake and threw them to the ground. Tea bushes sprung up from where they landed. The leaves kept him awake and so the myth goes, China had tea.

Notables 'Zen and the Art of Motorcycle Maintenance' by Robert Pirsig.

ZOROASTRIANISM
(PARSIISM)

- Monotheistic Classical Religion
- 1,200 BCE Iran, India & elsewhere
- Ahura Mazda The Wise Lord
- 200,000
- www.zoroastrianism.com

HISTORY

The prophet Zarathustra/Zoroaster started the religion in N.E. Iran after seeing the wholly good Ahura Mazda. It spread to become the first and second (Sassinid) Persian Empires' religion. With the growth of Islam its followers were persecuted, some emigrating to the religious freedom of India (Parses translates as 'of Persia'). Of late it is more tolerated by Islamic Iran, although numbers are dwindling.

BELIEFS

Ahura Mazda created an essentially good world. There is a continuing struggle between good (Spenta Mainya) and destructive evil (Angra Mainyu), where man has a personal responsibility to choose a side. Resurrection of the dead, a heaven and a hell exist. Good thoughts (Humata), works (Hukta) and words (Havarshta) sum up the credo.

POINTS OF INTEREST

Corpses Traditionally disposed of in Towers of Silence (Dakhmas) by exposure to the sun and vultures for ecological, theological and spiritual good.

Text The Avesta containing laws (Vendidad) hymns (Gathas) and prayers twice destroyed, once by Alexander the 'Great' or 'Accused'.

Guinness Book of Records States it is the most endangered religion.

Prayer After washing, five times per day in the presence of fire wearing a sacred cord (Kisti) and shirt (Sudreh) and never facing North.

Magi Priesthood famous for being the wise men that brought gifts to the infant Jesus in Bethlehem.

Marriage Marriage outside the religion is of late not allowed.

Fravahar The religion's symbol or guardian soul. Depicts the old man of wisdom ascending.

Judgement All dead cross the bridge of Chinvat to a Paradise of Songs or fall to be guests in the House of Lie.

Notables Farokh Engineer (cricketer), Freddie Mercury (singer), Feroze Gandhi (politician).

SOME RELEVANT WORDS MADE EASY

A GLOSSARY

ABSOLUTION religious statement of forgiveness for sin.

ADHERENT supporter or follower of a set of ideas.

ADVENTIST believer in imminent second coming of Jesus Christ.

AKA also known as.

ALLAH the Muslim God.

ALMSGIVING donation of money or food.

AMRIT a divine syrup; sweetened water for Sikh baptism.

ANABAPTIST rebaptisers who administer baptism to believing adults.

ANGEL spiritual being who acts as a messenger of god.

ANGLICAN member of or connected to the Church of England.

APOCALYPSE the total, final destruction of the world as in the Book of Revelation.

APOCRYPHA appendix to the Bible's Old Testament.

APOSTLE each of the twelve chief disciples of Jesus Christ.

ARMAGEDDON Biblical last battle between good and evil.

ARYAN invaders of India in c1,500BCE.

ASCETIC practice of severe self-discipline.

ATHANASIAN CREED Christian profession of faith on the Trinity and incarnation.

AUGSBURG PEACE recognition of Catholicism and Lutheranism as long as subjects follow the religion of their rulers.

AVALOKITESVARA a distinguished Buddhist Bodhisattva.

AYATOLLAH a Shiite Islamic religious leader.

BABYLONIAN inhabitant of Babylon, ancient city/kingdom in Mesopotamia.

BAPTISM rite symbolizing purification or initiation into a church often involving partial or total immersion in water.

BCE Before Christian or Common Era.

BEATIFICATION the first step to being declared a saint by the Pope.

BELIEF to hold a proposition to be true.

BETHLEHEM Village in Judah where Jesus Christ was born.

BIBLE Christian scripture.

BISHOP senior member of Christian church.

BODHISATTVA Buddhist able to reach nirvana, but who delays doing so through compassion for suffering beings.

BONISM a pre-Buddhist shaman religion.

BOOK OF CONCORD set of main documents of Lutheranism.

BOOK OF REVELATION the last book of the New Testament.

BRAHMAN Hindu supreme soul of the cosmos.

BUDDHA an enlightened being who has seen the truth of Dharma.

c about.

CALIPH successor of Muhammad or religious/civil leader.

CANAAN ancient land between Mediterranean and Dead Sea.

CANON set of genuine sacred books or large piece of military ordnance.

CANONISE Pope declares an heroic person (often dead) a saint.

CE Christian or Common Era

CELESTIAL heavenly.

CELT pre-Roman peoples of Europe and Asia Minor.

CHARISMATIC a divinely inspired Christian.

CHURCH building used for Christian worship. A specific religion.

CLASSICAL relating to ancient culture, especially Greek and Latin.

COENOBITE member of monastic community.

COMMUNION the practice of fellowship or specifically the Christian Eucharist.

CONFEDERATION a partnership of groups.

CONFIRMATION ritual of confirming members to a church.

CONFUCIANISM Chinese philosophy of Confucius.

COUNTER-REFORMATION Catholic fight back after Protestant reformation in 16C.

COVENANT solemn agreement specifically to God.

CREATION the creation of the universe.

CREDO a statement of a person's beliefs or aims.

CREED a system of religious belief.

CROSS upright wooden post with cross member on which Jesus Christ was crucified.

CRUCIFIX symbol of a cross bearing the figure of Jesus Christ.

CRUSADE religious military expedition.

CULT small religious group often perceived by outsiders as weird.

CURSE request a deity to cause harm to someone or something.

DEACON lowly ranking Minister of the Christian church.

DECUSSATE 'x' shaped.

DEITY a god or goddess.

DHARMA Hindu, Buddhist and Jain law or principle underlying social and physical life.

DIANETICS a system for the relief of psychosomatic disorders.

DIET OF WORMS conference at which Martin Luther was required to retract his teachings.

DISCIPLE a follower/pupil of a teacher.

DIVINATION predicting the future through occult means.

DIVINE of, from, or like a god.

DOCTRINE beliefs taught by a religion.

DOOMSDAY day of final judgement on last day of the world.

DORMITION feast in honour of the death of the Virgin Mary.

ECCLESIASTICAL of the Christian Church or its clergy.

ECUMENICAL representing a number of different Christian churches.

EMANATION the appearance of a deity.

ESOTERIC clear only to those with special knowledge.

EUCHARIST sacramental commemoration of the Last Supper.

EVANGELICAL fervent advocacy of Christian teaching, especially the authority of the Bible.

EVANGELIST someone trying to convince others of the Christian faith.

EXTRA-TERRESTRIAL being not of this world.

FAITH conviction of the truth of some doctrine.

G-d polite reference to God.

GIOTTO 13C Florentine painter.

GOSPELS first four books of the Bible's New Testament, Mathew, Mark, Luke and John.

GRAND MASTER the Freemason's head, who may be good at chess.

GREAT SCHISM either a split within the Roman Catholic Church or the split between the Orthodox Eastern and Roman Catholic churches.

HEATHEN a person who does not believe in a major religion.

HEAVEN house of god(s) and the good after death.

HEDONISM pleasure seeking.

HELL place of evil and suffering for the wicked after death.

HERESY a belief differing from mainstream religious principles.

HOLINESS MOVEMENT early charismatic Christian movement

of 19C America; believers expected physical healing and baptism of the Holy Spirit.

HOLY SEE the area over which the Pope has jurisdiction.

HOLY SPIRIT third person of the Christian Trinity.

HYMN sung praise of god.

ICON representative symbol that is worshiped, often a person or an object.

IDOL object of worship.

IDOLATRY idol not idle worship.

IMAM successor to Muhammad or leader of Islamic prayers in a mosque.

IMMANENT operating and present within the cosmos.

INSHALLAH if Allah wills it.

ISLAM religion of the Muslim peoples.

JEHOVAH name of Hebrew God.

JESUS CHRIST son of Christian God.

JUDAH biblical figure, then tribe, then ancient kingdom, capital Jerusalem.

JULIUS CAESAR Roman Emperor (14–37).

KARMA Hindu, Buddhist and Jain law of moral cause and effect.

KHALSA group of orthodox Sikhs.

KORAN sacred book of Islam containing the word of Allah.

LAST SUPPER meal eaten by Jesus Christ and his disciples on the night before his crucifixion.

LAY non-clerical.

LUCIFER the devil.

MANDALA Hindu and Buddhist symbol representing the universe.

MANNA food.

MANTRA devotional chant.

MARTYR one who is killed due to their religion.

MEDITATION focusing one's mind for spiritual aims.

MENNONITE followers of Menno Simons and successors of the Anabaptists.

MERKAVAH Jewish chariot.

MESSIAH actual/expected rescuer of an oppressed people.

MIDDLE AGES European period from c1,000 to 1,453.

MILLENARIAL Group believing in future 1,000 year millennium.

MISHNAH Jewish traditions and law and part of the Talmud.

MISSION travel abroad to spread a faith, either possible or impossible.

MISSIONARY one on a religious mission.

MONK member of male religious community.

MONOTHEISM doctrine that there is only one god.

MORTIFICATION domination of one's desires.

MOSQUE Muslim place of formal worship.

MOVEMENT group working together for a shared cause.

MUHAMMAD the last prophet of Islam.

MUSLIM an adherent of Islam.

MYSTICISM ancient religious mysteries or other occult rites.

MYTH legend regarding the early history of a people.

MYTHOLOGY a set of myths.

NEW AGE movement categorised by its alternative approach to Western traditional culture.

NEW TESTAMENT second part of the Bible. Record of the life and teachings of Jesus Christ.

NGO - non-governmental organisation.

NICENE CREED statement of Christian faith defending the Trinity.

NIRVANA Buddhist state of no suffering, desire or sense of self; perfect happiness.

NORSE peoples or language of Norway and Scandinavia.

OCCULT supernatural/magical powers, practices or phenomena.

OLD TESTAMENT first part of Bible, Genesis to Malachi.

OMNIPRESENT ever present everywhere.

ORDER a society living under the same rule.

ORDINATION lay person qualifying to holy orders.

ORTHODOX conforming to traditional beliefs.

PAGAN person following beliefs other than the main world religions.

PAPAL BULL decree from the Pope.

PARADISE a heavenly place.

PARISH church district.

PASTOR person responsible for a Christian church or congregation, not Italian food.

PATRIARCH title given to the head of a See.

PENANCE act performed as repentance of sin.

PENTECOSTAL emphasising baptism in the Holy Spirit, proved by speaking in tongues, prophecy, healing and exorcism.

PIETY characteristic of being devoutly religious.

PILGRIMAGE religious journey.

PLINY Roman author of Natural History, now understood to be a mixture of fact and fiction.

POLITICO political.

POLYGAMY practice of having more than one wife/husband at the same time.

POLYGYNY polygamy in which a man has more than one wife.

POPE head of Roman Catholic Church.

PRAYER thanks or request to a deity.

PRELATURE rank of ecclesiastical dignitary.

PRIEST ordained minister of a church.

PRIMATE provincial head bishop.

PROPHECY a prediction.

PROPHET foreteller or leader of a religion.

PROTESTANT a member of a non-Roman Catholic church which accords with the principles of the Reformation.

PSYCHIC one possessed of occult powers.

RABBI Jewish scholar, teacher or leader.

RADIONIC HEALING energy healing.

REDE advice.

REFORMATION 16C reform of the Roman Catholic Church leading to Protestantism.

REINCARNATE rebirth in another body.

RELIGIO of religion.

RELIGION system of faith and worship.

REPENT express or feel remorseful or regretful.

RESURRECTION Jesus Christ's rising from the dead or the rising of the dead at the Last Judgement.

REVELATION divine or supernatural disclosure.

REVERENCE profound respect.

RITE religious ceremony.

RITUAL a religious ceremony.

SABBATH day of religious observance and abstinence.

SACRAMENT Christian symbolic ceremony.

SACRED holy.

SACRIFICE act of killing or giving up a possession to offer a deity.

SAINT a virtuous person canonised after death.

SALVATION release from consequences of sin.

SANATANA DHARMA Hindu eternal truth.

SANSKRIT ancient language of India, used for religion and scholarship.

SATAN the devil.

SCHISM disagreement resulting in separation of a religious organisation.

SCRIPTURE sacred writings.

SEAL final prophet or aquatic mammal.

SÉANCE gathering where a spiritualist endeavours to contact the dead.

SECOND COMING the return of Jesus Christ.

SECULAR free of religious rule.

SEE the area over which a Christian bishop has authority.

SEMINARY college for priests.

SERMON talk given during a church service.

SHAMAN person with access to/influence in the spirit world.

SHARIA traditional law of Islam.

SHRINE holy place sometimes housing a religious icon.

SIN wrongdoing, particularly against religious law.

SOUL the spiritual part of a person often regarded as immortal.

SPIRIT the ethereal part of man that survives death.

SPIRITUAL regarding religious belief.

SPIRITUALISM belief centred on contact with the dead.

SUPERSTITION faith in supernatural power.

SUTRA Hindu and Buddhist scripture.

SUTTA dialogue of the Buddha.

SYNAGOGUE Jewish place of worship.

TALMUD Jewish law code containing the six Mishnahs.

TANTRA Buddhist or Hindu mystical or magical text.

TAWHID the defining principal of Islam.

THEISM belief in the existence of one or more gods.

THEOLOGICAL religious theory and beliefs.

THEOSOPHICAL SOCIETY society founded on ancient religious philosophy in 1875 by Helen Blavatsky.

THEOTOKOS title of the God-bearing Virgin Mary.

TOTEM an animal, vegetable or mineral with symbolic spiritual significance.

TRANCE a semi-conscious condition entered into by a medium.

TRANSCENDENT operating outside restrictions of the material cosmos.

TRINITARIAN relating to the doctrine of the Trinity.

TRINITY three persons of the Christian Godhead: Father, Son and Holy Spirit.

UFO unidentified flying object.

VALKYRIES Odin's warlike hand maidens.

VATICAN COUNCIL Roman Catholic general council.

VEDIC relating to ancient Hindu scriptures.

VENERATION reverence, worship, adoration.

VENIAL a pardonable sin as opposed to a mortal sin.

VENUS second planet of the solar system.

VICAR OF CHRIST the Pope.

VIKING 8-11C Scandinavian seafaring peoples.

VIRGIN MARY blessed mother of Jesus Christ.

WORSHIP formal or informal reverence of a deity.

YOGA discipline using breath control, meditation and specific postures.

ZION a heavenly place to which exiled peoples hope to return.

A LITTLE BIBLIOGRAPHY

A full list of sources is available at www.greatsects.com

Major sources and further reading

1,000 Great Lives	PS Fry	1975
A Concise Companion to the Jewish Religion	L Jacobs	2003
A Dictionary of Buddhism	D Keown	2003
A Dictionary of the Bible	WRF Browning	2004
A Popular Dictionary of Paganism	J Pearson	2002
Aborigine Dreaming	J Cowan	2002
Belief Beyond Boundaries	J Pearson	2002
Chambers Biographical Dictionary	M Magnusson	1990
Charts of Cults, Sects and Religious Movements	H Wayne House	2000
Christian Symbols	Dover Publications	2003
Collins World Religions	D Gill	2003
Encyclopedia of New Religions	C Partridge	2004
Guinness World Records 2004	C Folkard	2004
Hinduism A Very Short Introduction	K Knott	2000
Holy Bible King James Version	Cambridge	1927
Indigenous Religions	G Harvey	2000
Islam A Very Short Introduction	M Ruthven	2000
Islam for Dummies	Prof M Clark	2003

Shamanism Archaic Techniques of Ecstasy	M Eliade	2004
The Complete Idiot's Guide to Hinduism	L Johnsen	2002
The Concise Oxford Dictionary of the Christian Church	EA Livingstone	2000
The Concise Oxford English Dictionary	OUP	2004
The Encyclopedia of American Religious History	Queen/Prothero/Shattuck	1996
The HarperCollins Concise Guide to World Religions	M Eliade & I Couliano	2000
The Hutchinson Encyclopedia of Living Faiths	RC Zaehner	2004
The Mitchell Beazley Illustrated Biographical Dictionary	G Howatt	1977
The New Penguin Handbook of Living Religions	J Hinnells	1998
The Oxford Dictionary of Islam	JL Esposito	2003
The Oxford Dictionary of Popes	JND Kelly	2003
The Oxford Dictionary of Saints	DH Farmer	2004
The Oxford Dictionary of World Religions	J Bowker	1997
The Oxford Guide to People and Places of the Bible	B Metzger & M Coogan	2001
The Religions of Oceana	T Swain & G Trompf	1995
The World's Religions	N Smart	2003
The World's Religions	H Smith	1991
UFO Religions	C Partridge	2003

A LITTLE BIBLIOGRAPHY
CONTINUED

Online resources

http://en.wikipedia.org/
http://www.about.com/
http://www.adherents.com/
http://www.amazon.com/
http://www.angelfire.com
http://www.bbc.co.uk/religion/
http://www.beliefnet.com
http://www.britannica.com/
http://www.cia.gov/
http://www.globalsecurity.org/
http://www.godulike.co.uk/
http://www.google.co.uk/
http://www.nationmaster.com/
http://www.newadvent.org/
http://www.religionfacts.com
http://www.religiousmovements.lib.virginia.edu/
http://www.religioustolerance.org/
http://www.rickross.com/
http://www.sacred-texts.com
http://www.thinkexist.com/

AND FINALLY

What do you get if you cross a Jehovah's Witness (p. 60) with an Atheist (p. 30)?

Someone who knocks on your door for no reason.

THE SECTS INDEX

QUOTATION

'There is only one religion though there are a hundred versions of it.'

GB Shaw (Plays Pleasant and Unpleasant (1898))